read the information, talk to a coach or listen to the tapes you make, and then let it sink in. You are probably already doing most of the things that experts suggest. The key to this part of your training is to use it without spending much thought or effort on the skills. Just let it become part of your program and let it happen. Ultimately, you will want to enter a flow state: perform without even having a thought, and enjoy your activity.

Your choice

Positive benefits can result from actually training your mental skills. If you have doubts, talk to Olympic Medalists Dennis Hall, Matt Ghaffari, Kendall Cross or Kurt Angle. These athletes credit a positive, active mental skills program with assisting them in reaching the levels of success they were able to obtain. The interesting thing is that these men are totally different in their approach to a program! Each has a different wrestling style, different background, and different needs. Yet they were able to design personal programs that helped them develop the skills that they used in their training and in competition. And you can see the results. By deciding that mental skills were important, investigating the different methods they could use, then incorporating their selections into their program, these men became total athletes.

Mental skills will not make an elite athlete. It takes hard work, skills, dedication and good luck to get to the elite level. But mental skills training can add icing to the cake, making you a better competitor.

So, right now, decide to include a mental skills plan in your program. The sooner you get started, the more you will be able to accomplish. And remember, these are not skills for 'sick' athletes or athletes who are having problems. These are skills that any athlete can use. I teach the psychological skills that will enable you to enhance your training and competitions. They should be a part of every athlete's tool box!

Methods

You will be asked to use several different methods in your trip through this program. These methods will assist you in learning to understand and apply sound mental skills to your total program. This should make you a better, well-rounded athlete and help you reach or accomplish more of your competitive goals.

The first objective of this program is to point you in the right direction. This is done by teaching you specific skills and ideas. Many of these psychological concepts are easy to understand, it's just that sometimes we are afraid of the term psychology. We shouldn't be--psychology is just a science that looks at the ways we think.

You will be asked to read each section. Some of the sheets have lessons. Others have a lesson, and then an assignment. If you are working as a team, take some time to discuss the ideas. Allow all of the athletes and coaches to give their thoughts. We can always learn from others' experiences. If what they say makes sense, then let it soak in. If what they say doesn't make sense, you are forced to compare it to your beliefs. In doing this, you either reaffirm that your approach is right, or you decide to change it. So, either way, we can learn from discussing thing with other people.

Much of the written work is based upon the idea that it is beneficial to make plans. The major concept is that if you have mentally planned, then practiced the situations you will encounter in your matches, you will be ready to respond to these specific situations when they occur in your matches. If you think about it, that is the way we practice our physical skills. We practice moves that will work in certain situations. We drill them, and when that situation occurs we automatically respond with the moves we have committed to our muscle memory.

You will then be asked and encouraged to evaluate your plans. That means that you will look at what you have planned, and then decide if your plans fit what you actually need to do to be successful. There is really no right or wrong, but this program encourages you to look at the techniques and strategies which have been successful for a large number of teams and athletes in our sport, and then compare your approach to theirs.

Next, you will be asked to perfect your plans by practicing. Just like physical skills, mental skills can be improved by practicing them. This may be a new idea for many. Few of you have ever been asked to practice your mental skills, but with this program that will change.

Practice what you plan. Make it part of your total program. Learn the material so well that it becomes automatic--then you can perform without even thinking. That is when you will be at your best.

The last phase of the program will be for you to implement the plans. You will take what the program has given you, and you will just do it! Without a thought as to what you should do, you will just get into your performance and let it rip.

I mentioned written work and "lessons". These words turn some athletes off. Many people have a negative connotation with the idea of extra work, or of having to "learn". Hopefully, this program will not come across as a textbook. One of the concepts we talk about with our athletes is called 'framing'. *Framing* and *reframing* are the ideas that we can look at something from a different point of view. The point of view we take has a lot to do with how we feel about something--so look at this work as being beneficial to your wrestling. Frame it in that light.

Focus on what you learn instead of the little extra work you will have to do. Think of it this way--few athletes across the nation are getting the mental skills information and learning what you are getting by completing this program.

This workbook offers you a way of improving, but, you must make the commitment to do the work. If you read the material and think about it, you will grasp some of the ideas. If you actually go through the lessons, answer the short questions in your own words, and then think about what you wrote, you will really understand.

To maximize your results, read the material, think about it, make the plans it asks for, then practice the ideas. A coach or parent can help, or you can do it on your own. Success will depend on how well you understand and then think through the tasks. Learning will be enhanced by actually completing each task, and then applying the ideas to your daily performances. Ultimately, you'll want to "forget" the ideas and allow them to become part of your belief system.

So, right now, let me ask you some simple questions:
1) What do you want to know about mental skills and preparing for a match?
2) What have been some of your problems in this area in the past?
3) What have you done to help yourself?
4) What have the coaches shown you?
5) If I show you how, are you willing to do the work to find ways to become a better athlete?

Now go back and <u>write your answers</u> to these five questions. These should be <u>your</u> answers. Do you really mean it, or are you writing what your coaches or parents want you to write? Are you willing to do the work, or are you just posing? If you don't want to write, then you will be missing half of the benefits.

Is it a waste of time? I can't answer that, but I will say that three World Champs, two Olympic Gold Medalists, three other Olympic medalists, numerous National Champions and dozens of All-Americans have completed the same homework in the last few years. It helped them develop a mental skills approach that assisted them in reaching their levels. If they thought it was worthwhile, then what do you think?

Good luck. It'll take some effort, but the athletes who really want to be champions and the athletes who know what it takes will jump right into it and do the tasks.

Dennis Hall speaks

When I was in high school we practiced our techniques and moves. A lot of time was spent on the mat working on situations and live wrestling. Not much time was spent practicing mental skills.

At the matches, I would sit in the stands before I wrestled and my mind would wander. I would think about <u>his</u> favorite moves and actually try to figure out how to stay away from <u>his</u> stuff. Sometimes I would get nervous and wouldn't have a proper warm-up. I wasn't really able to focus on my stuff.

As I started wrestling at the elite level, I began thinking that I needed to work on my mental skills. In a tight match my mind would often start freaking. I would lose focus. The bottom line was, that for me to reach the level I dreamed of reaching, I needed to learn about mental skills and to work on them.

Meeting my perfect match

Back in 1994, I was introduced to a concept called the "perfect match". I believe it was this concept that helped me turn the corner in my wrestling career. Up until this point, my best world placing was 8th place in the 1992 Olympic games. Since I began using this concept, I have won three world medals, including a world title in 1995.

Coach Hendrix introduced me to the perfect match. I thought it was a good idea because I liked the idea of training my mind. I knew my wrestling had to be automatic, but I had to figure out how to make it automatic. Coach and I talked about the perfect match. He gave me a form that explained the idea and showed what he wanted. I decided to try it to see if it would help. My perfect match was designed to help build confidence in myself along with correcting some little problems I had been facing.

Writing it out

I began my perfect match by writing down some problem areas for me. My perfect match consists of two areas. The first area deals with developing a proper warm-up. I wrote down my warm-up step by step. It was very detailed, and this part of the perfect match deals with prematch jitters. I found out that by doing the same warm-up every time, you eliminate the negative thoughts that are going through your mind when you have a random warm-up.

The last part of the perfect match is much more detailed. The way I began writing it was by jotting down areas where I needed help during my matches. The general areas were: 1) Always make first contact. 2) Keep my hands moving (two on ones, head snaps, arm drags). 3) Remember to look at the coach's corner during any breaks. 4) Use positive self-talk (example: when put down in par tarre I'll tell myself my defense is the best in the world). 5) Include key words that you want the coaches to yell throughout the match (be physical, pick up the pace, he's tired). 6) Attempt my best move a couple of times.

After jotting down the thoughts, I began to put my perfect match together in a story form. I wrote my match out including every little detail. Next, I put the above areas where I needed help into a real match situation. I described a match where I felt confident and did everything that I needed to do in order for me to say it was a perfect match. I ended up winning 4-1. I chose to let my opponent score to make the match more realistic.

Coach Hendrix and I discussed what I had done. We wanted it to be positive and to include adversarial situations like a bad call by the referee, so I added a little to it. Coach then made a tape where he says my perfect match over music. I chose two of my rock favorites-- Queensryche and Ozzie, and Coach Hendrix added some others. It was about thirty minutes long.

Note from Coach Hendrix: Dennis has been gracious enough to even include some personal dialogue from his "perfect match" to allow us to see what an elite athlete really thinks or wants to think as he competes. The following sections are excerpts from his perfect match tape. It is my voice he hears on his tape, so we chose to use the third person by saying *"Dennis, you are"* or *"you feel"* to invoke his visualization and mental practice. In the following sections, "A Perfect Warm-up" and "My Perfect Match" *italicized* sections are the words that Dennis is hearing over the music. If Dennis had recorded the voice-over, he would have used the first person-- "I am" or "I will" for the dialogue. (Thanks, Dennis!)

A Perfect Warm-up

Dennis, let's get in a mood to wrestle. Take a deep breath. Relax. I want you to go back to a time when you were great. A time when you felt you were at the top of your game. Try to hear it, smell it, taste it and enjoy it. We are going to go through a warm-up, get ready for the match, and then practice a perfect match. So let's capture that feeling and let's do it!

The music starts and the dialogue begins. Bong, bong, bong. "Let's get ready to rumble!" *Great. See yourself running, skipping, tumbling and moving. It's time; time to get ready. You know how you like to run, you like to skip, like to get really, really, really fired up, start to moving and getting that sweat going. Stretching, getting that body ready. Time to transform from being a spectator into being a champion wrestler, to being a super athlete. It takes a little while. Transformation. Going from setting in the stands to being that package of dynamite with a short fuse.* Music plays a while to allow me to warm-up. *Running, skipping, tumbling, jumping--you know the routine--time to kick that butt, get ready.* The music plays some more. Coach talks and reminds me of certain ideas while I complete my first section of my warm-ups. *Great! Good job.*

Everybody dance now. Gonna make you sweat,....baby! Let the music take control! Let the rhythm move you! *Okay, now. You told me you like to have a little five minute match warming up. We like to push a little bit and warm-up. Get a real good sweat and blow it out. Imagine now you are with your partner. We gonna blow it out. We gonna get that five minute match in. Pushing-- pulling--moving. Great stance. Going to focus on tiring your partner out. Getting ready for battle. Feeling big. Getting ready. Going through that hard match. Pushing , pulling, moving. Motion, levels, corners. You know you work harder than anybody. You are in the best shape. You have just got to get ready! Take charge. Dominate. Push, pull, change levels, put your motion in, cut your corners.* More music plays as Coach adds reminders and affirmations. *You are in great shape, such great, great condition. Working harder than anybody. You are in such great shape. It's a rush knowing that. Pummel, cross pummel. You are baaaad. People hate working out with you 'cause you kick that butt.* Music allows me to get into my zone. *Getting into your zone. Getting into your flow state. Working yourself into a ready state.* Music for a while. *Pick up the pace for the last forty seconds or so. Pummeling, battling, smashing that head. Getting ready now. Great! Good job.*

A new song comes up. *It is about ten minutes before the match now, and you've got your plastics on. You are focusing on your pummelling skills. Maintain your position. Again Dennis, you are pummeling, pulling and snapping that head. Got your plastics on, trying to bust out that sweat. Change your balance point, change your level. Hot, nasty, slippery, wet. You've got your body covered with sweat. Working towards that perfect place, getting your body exactly ready.* Music and dialogue focuses me on reminders as the song plays on.

My perfect match
Now the rock and roll starts-- "Be the best you can". The tape now focuses me on my match thoughts. *"Dennis it's that time. You are ready for the match. Your warm-up has got you ready. You are perfect, ready. You are ready to battle, smash, pummel. It' s pouring out, the sweat. You are ready. You look at your coach. He towels you off. You turn. It's time. Time to show the world. Are*

you ready? Yeah. Are you tough? Yeah. Are you excited?
Hell, yeah. You can't wait. These are the moments you
have trained for. These are the moments you live for.

You shake hands. Get that feeling that you are ready
to dominate. Whistle blows. It's you on the attack. First
contact. Two on one. You shift to the head tie. Battling,
battling, battling, battling. First contact. Banging and
smashing. Constantly pushing. Pulling, rotating,
wearing him down.

He wants to fight. He starts out strong, but Dennis,
you know you are stronger. He can't maintain. He
adjusts. You drop your level. You pummel in and drag.
It's beautiful on the corner. You pound him. You pound
him. You pound him!

A section focuses on top technique: *He's got to give it*
up or back out. He jumps back. Hands come up on the
officials. Great--a passivity, your choice. You center
yourself, come back to the center and think about what
you want to do. He's down, you're ready, you're focused,
you are ready to attack. Hands together. Whistle blows,
you lock up a good lock. You go for a ....

Another section reminds me of certain things: *You*
go out of bounds and the whistle blows. Back to the
center. You run back and take your position. Ready.
Ready to wrestle. You are first back in the center, take a
breath and you are ready. Hustle back. Make the referee
see you are wanting to go. Make him want to call the
match your way. Look to your coach.

Training for bottom: *You have control. He's frozen.*
You have him so tied up that he can't move. But, they
caution you! You had him so tied up he couldn't move,
but they decided to put you down. That is okay. Again
you're in your zone, you focus, you center yourself. You
know what you have got to do. Focus on good defense.
Active on bottom. Moving. He can't score. I won't let him.
I am ready for anything he has. He's on top. He tries to
get a lock but you fight, you crawl, you've glued your
hips to the mat. It is a battle. He tries, to no avail, your
par tarre defense is just too strong. Moving, fighting,
crawling, hips to the ground, there's just no way.

Later in the match: *Your opponent begins to show some concern. You notice it in his eyes, you hear his breathing. You sense his fear. Pummelling, controlling, taking charge, that's the Dennis Hall way. Great. Coach yells, "pick up the pace." You understand. Whistle blows, first contact, again it's first contact, first contact. Strong, dominating, snap that head, great stance, great position, pummelling strong.*

Finishing the match: *Look at your coach. You refocus. Whistle blows. Again, Dennis Hall makes first contact. Beautiful, great position. Great movement, great motion. You hear him breathing and that's a key. It tells you that he is about to give up. If you can just be stronger for a little while longer. And you have it in you. You suck down deep into your conditioning and there you are. Pounding and kicking that butt. Listening to your opponent breathe, listening to your opponent struggle. Good motion, taking charge, looking big, looking good. Nothing can stop you now. Keeping a great head about you. Keeping position on the mat. Back to the center. Let him drift into the zone. Always, always fighting; always pummelling. You grind him. You make him want to give up. The more you hear him breathe, the better shape you are in. He's desperate and that makes you bigger and better.*

More music plays. *Fifteen seconds left. They caution you. That's okay. In your mind you know that's okay. You have just got to be tough. You focus. Active defense. Get a good start. Moving, fighting, battling elbows, crawling. He'll not get you up. You battle. You stop his first move as you fight. You battle and stay active. He slowly dies as time ....runs......out! Great job!*

The last song on my tape plays as Coach goes over and reinforces several points we have decided are important.

Its affects

Perfect match training helped me change how I look at things--how I, what we call "frame" my thinking. Now I concentrate on my match and my moves. I figured out that I can't defend everything, and anyway, I am the one who has to score the points, so I focus on what I can do, not what he does. This helped me get my thoughts together as far as mental skills go. I learned to believe that I should win every match, and I was able to make my mind as strong as my body.

"Practicing" mental skills

I usually practice by listening to my tape about a half hour before I go to bed. I have even listened to my match as I drove around in my truck. Last year I listened a lot, but this year I slacked off some, and now I regret it. I can honestly say I wish I had listened to it more before the Olympics. I think about five times a week is about right. I am going to listen to my new tape more and get back on it. I think that will help me get ready for this year.

In matches

My perfect match has kept me comfortable in several close matches. Last year in the World Championships I was behind by three with about twenty-five seconds left. My opponent, Yaldiz, was a World Champion. My perfect match had included my opponent scoring on me (although it did not include me being behind), so I was not that bothered. In my perfect match tape I drop my level and hit a high dive to score. *Boom, there it is.* Against Yaldiz, I knew I needed to score quickly, so I dropped my level and shot. That was the highest percentage move, so I hit it. *Boom, there it was.* He fell to his back and was stuck. I never panicked or freaked out. It just happened without me really thinking. I just did it.

Using affirmations

After I became comfortable with the perfect match, I began to work on including affirmations with my plan. (*Coach's note:* Affirmations are positive statements that build confidence and motivate. *"I am ready to battle when I step on the mat"*, *"I am in great shape and I grind people into the mat"* would be examples of Dennis' affirmations.) I think affirmations helped me by making me believe in my abilities. You know, what the mind hears, the body believes. There is nothing stronger than a good mind.

I have a list, and I read them at night. I think that to be the "best in the world" you must think you are the best. Sometimes we forget that, and the affirmations help remind me.

Fatigue control

Our last step was adding fatigue reduction and pain control to my match. This is where we worked on learning to control my thinking about pain and fatigue. In a match, you have got to go. You have just got to do it. You must learn to control pain and fatigue. Once I got serious, I was able to learn to control this. I learned to crumple the pain up and throw it over my shoulder, or make it smaller until it disappeared. I also learned to just say it wasn't there--to deny it, not let it affect me. It works. I never felt tired in my matches.

What's next

I plan to rewrite my perfect match--to do another tape. I'm currently developing a perfect match where I have to deal with adversity. I need to gather a plan of attack when things are not going my way. For example, I want to know how I'm going to come back from a four point deficit like what happened to me at this year's Olympics Games.

I want to focus on adversity--knowing the match is not over if I get behind. If I am behind by less than three, I'll beat him down and win. If I'm behind by four, I want to focus on cutting it down a point at a time. I just need to figure out what I want to do.

The warm-up is perfect, but I have a new song I want to add. We will get together and do my new one, and then I'll start listening to it.

Learning the "perfect match" system has really helped me. I plan to continue to use it--to become a

TERMINATOR. Tear my leg off, I'm still coming. Burn me, I'll still be after you. I'm going to get you. Everything is in automatic, and I'll be totally focused on what I want and need to do!

(This article first appeared in the March 1, 1997 Wrestling USA Magazine. Since it was published I have received many positive comments about the method.)

Now, go back and reread Dennis' story. Relax. Take a breath. Imagine you are Dennis. Turn into Dennis and feel his attitude. Capture his feeling. Imagine the music. See and feel yourself compete, dominating your opponent. This is what we are looking for-- learning to plan your match, practice it, and develop a comfortable approach to competing.

Then you implement the program (without thinking). You learn to warm-up, just right. Get into your zone. Become one with yourself and perform in automatic. Just like in practice. No worries. No thoughts. No breaks in concentration. You become a machine and perform. Optimum. Perfect. Out of sight!

Then, sometimes after the match, you will realize-- YOU WERE SMOKING! Wow! What a feeling!

Section I

Initial Focus

Making a plan of action, and then selecting the thoughts that will help you to fulfill your plan is not difficult. You just need to learn some basic skills before you begin. The first skill is goal setting, a process that most "sport psych" books discuss. That's because goal setting is a good starting place. It gives the athlete a destination and some direction as to the route he will take to get there. By selecting his destination and a route to get him there, the athlete has already begun planning his trip.

The second skill is called self-talk. This is the idea that we think or have discussions with ourselves. These discussions pave the way for our attitudes and the way we look at things. Our self-talk also gives us many clues as to our focus, goals, commitment and our way of thinking.

Read what Dennis and Matt say about their matches. Each thinks differently, yet their words can give you several clues to their way of thinking about competition. Which one do you more closely resemble?

"Pound their head. I want to make him give up, to mentally break my opponent. If I start out at full speed in the first two minutes, he will start to feel it. Keep pouring on the pressure." **Dennis Hall, 1995 Greco World Champion, 1996 Olympic Silver Medalist**

"I get ready for my match. I plan what I want to do, tell myself what to think, and then walk on the mat and do it." **Matt Ghaffari, 1995 World Cup Champion, 1996 Olympic Silver Medalist**

What they say about mental skills

Mental skills! The concept has been with us for centuries. Ancient athletes knew they had to be mentally prepared to perform. Many of them even meditated before they competed. But, until recently, coaches and athletes didn't focus their training on mental skills. For some reason everyone admitted that mental skills were important, but little was done to work on these skills.

But now, the tide is changing. Many of our top coaches are incorporating mental skills training into their programs. Let's see what they are saying.

"Talent and skill are important contributors to achievement in sport, but I don't think they are the most important factors. So many highly successful athletes exist today who are not gifted or who have not achieved mechanical perfection. They are everywhere in sport. So, what is the critical factor in wrestling achievement? It is called TOUGHNESS!"

"Toughness is the ability to consistently perform at a high level no matter what the competitive circumstances are. No matter what happens, no matter what is thrown at you, no matter what adversity you are faced with, you will still be able to bring all of your talents and skills to life on demand."

"Toughness is learned. Make no mistake about it. It is acquired the same way skills are. If you don't have it, it just means you haven't learned it yet. Anyone can learn it at any stage in their life."

"In a wrestler's preparation, mental skills training is as important as any technical or physical training. For the total package, one needs to be strong in all areas of wrestling. When the technical, physical and psychological all come together as one, now you are on to something." Steve Fraser, Olympic Gold Medalist and US National Greco Coach.

"Developing the basic mental skills is a prerequisite to becoming a champion. It is not enough to simply prepare the body for maximum performance. Getting "psyched" before a match is a short term fix that will fail against an opponent that is totally prepared. Even the wrestler who has a vast knowledge of holds and techniques is lost without mental preparation. The foundation of every athlete's basic training should include a regimen of consistent psychological schooling." Dan Chandler, Greco World Team Coach, and Olympic Team member.

"Mental skills training is the hidden edge in developing a wrestler...it is the eighth basic skill. You can't develop a total wrestler, a true champion, without this important foundation." Doug Reese, Women's World Team and successful college coach.

"As a coaching educator, the most frequently asked question I get from coaches centers around the psychological development of their athletes. Mental skills training is one of the most overlooked, yet critical components of successful athlete development. With it, athletes quickly separate themselves from the masses. Without it, becoming a world class athlete will remain elusive." Brett Penager, USA Wrestling Coaches Education Director.

"I feel mental skills training is a must to get to the next level toward the world medals. At the Olympic level, each wrestler is both physically and technically ready through coaching and hard training. It' the mental side that will help him overcome any negative obstacles that might occur. Why do you see year after year, the same world medalists perform? My answer is, they believe they are the best in the world." Rob Hermann, 1996 US Olympic Coach.

Choosing your road

Will you follow through on your mental skills training? That is something that you will have to think about. You read what Dennis said about his "Perfect Match" training. You read what some of the top coaches say about mental skills. Now, you must decide if it is worth your time.

What will you say? We often find that it is easy to say we will do something, but it's much harder to follow through on a long-term or time consuming commitment.

I learned a great technique in my counseling methods class. It is one that I often use when I talk to athletes about their actions. A wise counselor told us that we can use the analogy of a television set to investigate whether our client is really working toward affective change. He said that a client's story of action is much like a TV show-- there is sound and there is a picture to every story.

So, first, I can hear what you are saying. I hear all of the good ideas, and I hear what you say you will do. Yes, it sounds great! You will do this and you will do that. And if you do, then you will move much closer to success. Unfortunately, I only hear the words.

There is another item I need to check if I want to 'view' the progress you are making. We'll turn down the volume on the TV and see what the picture shows us about your doings.

If I can see you doing the actions, then I know they are getting done. The old saying that 'actions speak louder than words' is really true. If I see my athletes doing their assignments, if they bring in written Perfect Match plans, if they make me a list of affirmations, then I know they are thinking about their mental skills and are moving closer to gaining control of that portion of their skills triangle.

If I don't see action and just hear talk, then I am not sure. They may or may not be complying.

So, take a look at your TV program. What are the words? What does the picture show? It is your choice!

Setting Goals

There is a lot written about goal setting. It is often promoted as a magic way to achieve. But to really simplify the concept--all goal setting does is make a map for our progress. It gives us a final destination and allows us to develop a route to reach that point. Most of us will agree that it is easier to get some place if we know where we are going!

Long term and short term goals

Long term goals are destinations. You set long term goals to give you a focal or final point, and then you work toward reaching that point. Your work-outs and plans are based on reaching certain levels of readiness for competitions. You use these levels as long term goals and constantly move toward them.

Short term goals are the routes you take to get to your destination. Some people call them "baby steps" because they lead up to obtaining the final or long term goals. These goals should be less formal and should be changed if they are not effectively contributing to the process of reaching your long term goals.

All goals should be *challenging, realistic, specific* and *self-referenced.* You should also start making your goals performance-based instead of outcome-based. (Set goals based on what you can control. You can't control results. You can only control what you do, so set your goals based upon the number of times you will do something or the attempts you will make, but not on beating another person or team.)

Using goals

With these ideas in mind, we can use goal setting for several things. First, goals become our mission. We set the stage for success by setting a long term goal that we want to reach. Second, we can use our goals as a motivational factor. Ultimately, we want to reach our long term goals. To do this we must set goals and then commit to performing all of the short term tasks that we need to complete in order to reach that goal. Third, we can use our goals as a focal point. We actively focus on what we want to do. We plan our steps, focus on their completion, and work to reach that final destination.

Reaching goals

The ultimate long term goal is to reach your goals! Each day decide what you want to do. Take a moment to organize your thoughts, basing your day's activities on short term goals that will move you toward the final goals. Instead of just going through the day in automatic, think about what you want to accomplish, and then work to get there.

As you go through the day, evaluate what and how you are doing. Then accept and affirm that what you are doing is right, or take steps to change your approach. The trick is in learning to go through this process without spending much energy thinking about what you want to do. Make it a part of your daily routine. Forget the attitude of "today I have to, or ought to, or should do". Just get up, take a breath, and then think about what would be best. Some people like to make lists of what they want to do. If this helps, then get a small notepad and make your list. You can do the same thing in practice. Take a moment to focus on what your goals are for each activity. Then do the things it takes to reach that immediate short term goal. And be sure to reward yourself as you reach each goal!

By taking a moment to reward yourself for reaching your short term goals, you are reinforcing your motivation to complete your other goals. Many of us get so caught up in our long term goals that we don't take time to enjoy it when we successfully reach these short term ones. It doesn't have to be a big reward. Just take a moment and congratulate yourself, or give yourself a little pat on the back. As the old saying goes--Take some time to smell the roses.

Self-talk

(Building a winning dialogue)

From experience and research, we know that most athletes "talk" to themselves before, during, and after competition. Some of these thoughts help performance, while others hurt. This is normal. We are always thinking about things and working to protect ourselves. The trick is to move away from negative and to focus on the positive. As an athlete you must learn to focus on what you feel you need to do. If problems occur, find the solutions to these problems. Successful athletes learn to control their self-talk. They focus on the positive or on the task and get the job done!

Enhancement dialogue

Some athletes have developed a set of words or phrases they use that helps them to focus on what they want to do, or on technical ideas they want to remember. Common cues you may already use are: "Head" for keep your head in the right position, "elbows"--keep them in close to the body, "motion" to remind yourself to keep moving, "active defense" to keep yourself moving in par tarre, or "now" to trigger yourself to throw or shoot. It is interesting to note that athletes often use the words their coaches use as cues!

Cues

Make a list of the mental cues you use during your match. Describe when you would use them. Are there any other reminders or thoughts that you want to build into your match dialogue? *Your list:*

Problem recovery dialogue

There are common problems that can occur during a match. We know that these problems might occur. Many athletes learn to build a self-talk dialogue to use when these predictable problems arise. Examples: Bad call, stalling, complimentary passivity against you, or even mystery points. These situations arise and can cause a total disruption in your thinking. By designing a coping statement and then practicing it, you can train yourself to overcome the mental effects of a bad break.

Problem solving self-talk

What are some common problems that might occur during your match? What have you thought in the past? What do you want to say now?

List your predicted problems, and the self-talk you can use to combat them.

Problem   **Solution**

The key to using this method is to practice. Learn to think the thoughts that would first enter your mind when you hit a negative situation. Then practice shifting to your solution dialogue. Once you have completed this first assignment, you are on the road to understanding how to plan and how to implement a winning approach to wrestling!

Kurt Angle gives us a good example of problem solving. Kurt wanted to start scoring earlier in his matches so he thought about what he needed to do to address this concern. *"I wanted to become more intense because I didn't want to be caught behind. I wanted to have the lead. European wrestlers are hard to play catch up with."*

"I developed that approach (score quickly and get early flurries started*)--but at first, I was too eager and was stepping into stuff--so I started having an aggressive but controlled approach. I accomplished by consistency-- always working on it, and believing it would happen even if it didn't work for a while. I stuck to my plan."*

Matt Ghaffari spent many moments planning his matches and warmups. He used his affirmation work and really enjoyed listening to a perfect match tape that he wrote. He was prepared for the 1996 Olympics and performed well. His greatest challenge came in the finals as he faced the Russian Alexander Karelin. Battling all the way, Matt came up short, 1-0, in overtime. It was Karelin's closest match ever in international competition.

Photo by Doug Reese

Section II   **Meet your match**

1) Preparing for a match
2) Individual differences
3) Enhance performances by planning
4) Introduction to perfect matches
5) Suggestions and strategies
6) Adverse situations
7) More on your perfect match
8) Evaluating your plans

The crowd is crazy--cheering, moving, screaming. Everyone is out of their chairs. Flags are flying, people are waving their arms, and a feeling of energy seems to suck you up off your feet. It will make you stand! If you are not standing it is because you have passed out from the excitement.

There's a low rumble. No one knows exactly where to look, but suddenly someone sees the escort and the wrestler. Without a word, everyone senses the direction and turns to watch, no, not to watch, they want to be a part! An American wrestler bursts into the arena, arms pumping as fast as my heart. He's asking the crowd for support. Looking into the stands, he searches for that energy and pulls some of it down. He's in his zone!

If you weren't there, you missed it.

I can still feel the sensation, and it is a strong, emotional feeling. USA versus the world. Kendall Cross. Kurt Angle. Terry Brands. Townsend Sanders. Matt Ghaffari. Brandon Paulson. Dennis Hall. Bruce Baumgartner. They all brought that excitement into the arena with their medal matches and the wrestling community will talk about that special feeling for years to come.

It was time! Time for their perfect match, and they needed it. What suspense, what tension, what excitement! This was certainly a time when an athlete needed to perform without thinking.

Preparing for a match

Most of you have been on the mat before, and you think you know how to prepare for a match. Realistically, some of you do. For those athletes who feel like they are doing well, keep up the good work. You don't need to fix it if it <u>ain't</u> broken!

For the athletes who want to know more about match preparation, research shows us that there are some common ties among the most successful wrestlers. They appear to loosely follow the same patterns of mental skill applications. I have compiled an outline of suggestions (from this research and from personal experiences with my athletes) that will help put you on the right trail. Read these suggestions, compare them to what you are presently doing, and then affirm your preparation methods or make any needed adjustments.

Prematch nervousness

One thing that shows up in interviews with any wrestlers, both elite level and beginners, is the fact that many of them suffer from prematch anxiety. This is normal. When I talk to you about your preparation, you mention this, and you are not sure how to handle these feelings or if they are even affecting your performances. As long as this nervousness is not causing you to have focus problems, it is okay. It may even help activate you and keep you sharp, so, don't worry about a little tension. Accept it as part of the sport.

Preparation hints! A wrestler should:
1. Become self-centered. Focus on what you need.
2. Develop a plan of action based on what you want to do. (Plan a perfect match.)
3. Understand that there may be developments in a match that are unexpected and even unfair. Have a plan of action in mind for: Bad calls, complementary passivities against you, fleeing the mat, uncalled slips, or any other negative events.

4. Work to achieve that optimum feeling of readiness. Some athletes try to get really pumped up for a weaker opponent, and then they try to calm down for a tougher foe. Research tells us that the most successful athletes have an optimum arousal point. They achieve a feeling of readiness that tells them--it's time, time for anyone! "My body is ready." The roller-coaster effect of getting pumped up, or of having to calm down, is just too hard to handle. Work to reach your point of readiness each time.

5. Focus on appropriate topics.
6. Rid yourself of any negative self-talk that occurs.
7. Hit your *zone* or *flow state*.
8. Step on the mat. Become a wrestler. Clear your mind of outside concerns and focus on your plan.
9. Perform.
10. Recover from unexpected events. (Use your plan B.)
11. Enjoy your performance.

Kurt, what do you do for warm-ups? What do you think?

"Breathing techniques to relax. I try to stay relaxed so my reflexes are ready. I think about winning--repeatedly telling myself 'I am the best.' I say a prayer, jog to warm-up, stretch, drill and keep on a sweatshirt and or a t-shirt that has a lot of meaning to me (it was my dad's)."

Kurt proudly wears his Olympic Gold Medal. Looking at Kurt, its easy to see that he trained hard. What's not so easy to see is the mental skills training that he put into his program.

photo courtesy of Kurt Angle

Individual differences

Scholars and writers are fond of using research results as a foundation for their theories. Research says this and research says that. Yes, it is true that we can learn a lot about Joe Average from looking into research. Unfortunately, no one fits the composite picture of Mr. Average. So, what do we do? We take this research information and use it as a basis to form individual plans for our athletes.

It is hard for a coach to know how to approach every athlete. Each one is different, so no coach knows how to work with everyone. To best address this problem, we must turn to you. You know more about yourself than anyone else, and you are the expert on what you need. In keeping with that idea, we want to know how you get ready, what you need to get prepared, and how we can help? Then your coaches can use their experience paired with some research to offer you suggestions, techniques or ideas.

Your performance
How do you get ready to perform?
Do have a prematch routine? (This is commonly called a "RITUAL".)
  How long before your match do you start?
Do you want someone to help you during your routine?
  If so, what kind of help do you want?
Do you want to know your opponent's tendencies? (A scouting report)
Do you want to have positive encouragement?
Do you want to talk to people or have someone screen you away from other people?
Do you have a specific person that works best with you?
What, if anything, has given you the most problems in the past?

When was your best performance?
  How did you prepare for it?

When was your worst performance?
  How did you prepare for it?

   Think about your needs and how your coaching staff or support group can help. Is there anything you feel they can do that will assist you in preparing for your competition?

Now, scribble some thoughts you would like to think in your matches. Just write down some of the ideas or key thoughts you want to have.

Enhance performance by planning!

The major causes of stress are uncertainty of outcome, fear of failure, and worrying about the expectations of others. Two of these are directly related to planning. If we can construct a plan of action, we can often defeat the stress that is brought about by these concerns. We can learn to take away that uncertainty and work around the fear of failing.

What you ask for

In working with wrestlers over the course of the last decade, they have mentioned three time periods where they wanted the most help: 1) warming up, 2) immediate prematch, and 3) during the match. This makes sense. The closer we are to the competition, the more we worry!

Warm-up and immediate prematch

Wrestlers' number one concern appears to be prematch anxiety. For some, prematch is a time of stress. Others say they don't know what this time is. They waiver between "feeling okay" and being lost. That is common among athletes. In every sport I work with, the athletes tell me this. The key is in learning to focus on what you do and what you control. Several of our most successful wrestlers have learned to control this by developing a ritual that includes a planned dialogue. Yes, there are wrestlers who write a script to think during their warmup. They then learn this script and focus on it during their prematch ritual. By having this time already planned (and their head already full of programmed thoughts) they are able to stay focused on what they actually want to do. They don't have the time to worry; they are too busy thinking helpful thoughts!

During the match

Most of you can get into your match after the first series. There tends to be a lot of stress until first contact, and then your focus changes. Then, usually you will be able to forget about the stress and start to function at an acceptable level. But a good number of you tell me you have "gone blank", "got frustrated", had no idea of strategy, or even "started getting pissed" during the match. These things happen, but they happen more often to people who do not have a good feel for their match strategy or to those who have not trained properly.

Another major concern that often I see is the fear of fatigue. This fear is one that is experiential in nature. Most of us who have been on the mat know what it is to run out of gas or "suck a little wind". It is not a good feeling, so we want to avoid it. Unfortunately, this fatigue will occur often in our matches, especially in close ones against tough competition.

Many of these situations can be somewhat controlled by planning your dialogue. That is simple enough, but it takes some time and commitment to go through the steps. Controlled self-talk is a blessing to the athletes who can achieve it, so I want you to work hard to perfect that skills.

An interesting point on fatigue/pain control has been discovered. Research tells us that if you just understand that you have the ability to control pain, you can begin to control it. But be careful. Pain is a warning, telling us something is wrong. Yes, you can actually learn to ignore or control the fatigue pain that comes along with exertion, but you can cause problems or greater injury if you begin to ignore injury pain. The key is to learn to block your "fatigue pain" and control your focus. To do this you must practice becoming fatigued and then work on it while you are tired.

Practice:

1) Swooshing it. Make it smaller, then toss it away.

2) Relabeling it. Call it something else.

3) Delaying it. You can hurt three minutes later.

4) Denying it. Tell yourself it is not there.

5) Liking it! This is how you like to feel! It means you are working hard and he is feeling even worse.

Introduction to perfect matches

What do you do when you are called to the mat? What
do you think about? What do you say to yourself? What is
your match strategy? Many athletes have learned these
concepts experientially. That means that they were
never actually taught how to think before or during their
matches. Their coaches just left it up to the athletes to
learn by trial and error.

Yes, athletes can learn from experience.
Unfortunately, this trial and error program leaves a lot
to be desired, and some athletes never learn the correct
way. They are the ones who must suffer. Many of them
have the physical ability and the coaching to succeed, but
they just can't seem to get it together.

Problems

Some go blank when they step onto the mat. Others
feel lost. Some even become worried about their foe, or
may go into a funk. A few even end up using wrong
strategies. Again, these are common occurrences. Yes,
they are negative and don't help your performances, but
they are common. So, what can we do to help our
performances?

Some solutions

Start by thinking your way through a perfect, hard
fought match. Make sure it covers all aspects of your
match. (Top, bottom, feet, match strategies)

Now write your perfect match.

After you have constructed a good match,
A) Identify problems that might occur.
B) Find solutions to these problems. Make *If, then statements*. (If this happens, I'll do this.)

Write some of these statements, and then write your solutions.

Learn it
Make it become a part of your thinking--
Train yourself to go into automatic and get into a response set. Spend time seeing yourself be successful. Think about your perfect match, what you want to do, and how you will react in every situation.

As I said--Practice it. Read it. Say it. Listen to it. Learn it. Master it. Let it become automatic.

Olympic Gold Medalist Kendall Cross believes you should practice a technique until you master it.
"Shooting on your opponent needs to be automatic, or, for lack of a better word, instinctive. So I drilled my shots over and over again in the practice room to develop an automatic response. If you have to consciously think about shooting on your opponent, there's a real good chance you will miss the window of opportunity. I believe you need to drill your shots repeatedly to create a natural flow of technique. I also feel it is important to drill you shots all the way to the mat in order to make your finishes 'automatic' as well."

Suggestions and strategies

There are ideas and strategies that will help a wrestler work through a tough match. In scholastic wrestling the most noticeable strategy we must consider is position choices at the end of the periods. How do you make these choices? There are probably no right or wrong choices, there are just situations that require you to be in a "best possible" position. So, first, let's take a look at some strategies behind making choices in a tough match.

Your style

The first consideration should be your personal style and strengths. Where are you the most comfortable? What do you do best? Many wrestlers have total confidence in their skills and have no problem making a choice. If they have a record for most takedowns in a season, they will probably want to wrestle on their feet. If they have the best cradle in the world, top is their choice. If their switch is a killer or they have a good roll, then they may feel comfortable on bottom. That makes sense. You will most likely want to go with your style and make your foe fight your match.

Situations

How is the match going? Have you turned him twice in the last thirty seconds? Has he ridden you? Have you been dominant on your feet? Continue the momentum if it is going in your direction. If your opponent has momentum, change the flow by choosing the position that stops or reverses his attack. Dariel Daniel (National High School Athletic Coaches Association "Coach of the Year") says, "If I have seen a definite mismatch in one of the areas, say I have three takedowns and he has none, or I have turned him twice in the first period, I will want to keep that going. The takedown man would choose neutral, while the turner would choose top."

What's the score? This is especially important in the third period. Is the match tied? Can you score from bottom? With the score tied or within one point, many people choose bottom in the third period. They feel that they can escape and tie or go ahead. This is an effective strategy, especially in high school where there is no riding time.

Most athletes feel they can get up from bottom, but there are a couple of thoughts that you might want to consider before you make this choice. Has your foe been successful in riding you? Is he a leg rider? Have you been able to control him on the mat? How did you do while you were on your feet? What kind of shape are you in? How about him? If you feel you have a good chance to escape and make it close, tie, or take the lead, then do it! You have to do what you have confidence in. You are the one who has to do the hard work.

Your coach may help with your choice. Ron Gray, coach of Dowling High School (Iowa State Champions 1990-93), says, "I evaluate the flow of the match, and then balance that with my athlete's ability level and style. I want him to look my way at the break, and I will offer him a suggestion based upon what I have seen."

The strategy to defer brings the most debate. Some coaches feel it is best to take charge of a match and choose your best position. Others take a more cautious attitude and defer to the next period. If you are doing what you are supposed to, you may never see your opponent's best series because you can tech him or get a fall. Some people say, "Why give him a chance to dominate?" So, unless there is an overwhelming reason, make your choice based upon what you feel will best serve your purpose.

Practice

Practice making choices. Think about why you are making each selection. It is hard for younger athletes to understand these guidelines, but with discussion and practice, they soon learn to make a preliminary choice, and then look for the coach's suggestion. Practice this daily. Stop during practice to think, "What should I choose?" Ask your coach and have a discussion. There are no absolute right choices, only selections that are based on momentum, skills, situations, and mathematical odds. And these are open to debate. You must be able to apply these loose ideas to your personal style, match situation, and coach's philosophy.

One thing is for certain: You should plan for these situations in advance. Know when you would like to choose one position or the other. The referee will only give you a couple of seconds to make the call. Look quickly to your coach, get his input, and then make your decision. You may not agree with the reasons or selections stated above. That's okay. By thinking about your options you will assist yourself in developing a plan to use in your match. So, next time the ref looks your way and says, "Top, bottom, neutral or defer?" you will be ready with an intelligent and logical answer.

Strategies

Do you have match strategies? Do you have a certain way that you wrestle in specific situations? When you have two takedowns in the first period and it is your choice in the second, what will you do? When the score is tied and you are starting on bottom with twenty seconds left, what will you do?

You know you must pace yourself for the whole match. You must be able to go the distance. Yes, you will be able to beat the fish, but what about the studs? So, train your pace. Include pulsing. Think something like: "aggressive start, take control, explode with motion and level changes into a flurry, battle, return to strong position, recover, explode again".

Some other ideas:

1) Good stance and position are key points. Coaches say that getting in good position, looking more aggressive and winning the fight seems to be very important. Include motion and level changes statements in your thinking or match dialogues.

2) Bottom or par tarre defense is paramount. Today's scarcity of takedowns leaves us little room to give up

points on the mat. Refusing to give up on bottom will greatly increase your chances for victory. How long can you hold your hand in fire? How long can you fight for your life on bottom? It becomes a mental game! Then the next step is learn to score from bottom.

3) Score from top. There is that breaking point where your foe will give in. Push him to that point and make him cry for momma. It is not as important to him as it is to you, so put him in a position that encourages him to quit. Remember, it takes two takedowns to overcome one three point nearfall.

4) Unbalance your foe and attack with high percentage, low risk techniques. Keep up the pressure to encourage passivity calls or stalling against your foe. Spank him. Control him. Close him down. Make it unenjoyable for him to be on the mat with you.

5) Use our great conditioning to tire your foe. This will be to your advantage, especially late in the match, as his lungs burn, his legs get weak, and his arms get tired. You will be fresh and get a thrill in knowing he is getting ready to fold.

Special tactics for international styles:

A) Develop a rapport with the officials.

B) Continue to wrestle two seconds after the whistle.

C) Wrestle through the zone, into the safety area.

D) Play the game. Look like you are aggressive and act like you are in shape. Make the official want to support you and your style. No, make the official admire you and your wrestling technique and style. You can pick up extra points or help the ref see your side of the story with these tactics!

Adverse situations

There are times when things just do not go right. Stuff happens! Even the best laid plans can go astray. What does an athlete do when these things occur? Unfortunately, we find these situations can make the difference in being a champion or being an also-ran. A lot depends on how you respond to the situation.

What might go wrong?

Each of us probably has a nightmare story about something that just went wrong during a match or competition. What is yours? Could it have been corrected?

Make a list.

Make sure to think about all of the things that could go wrong. You can include things that happened to you, things that have happened to your friends. things you have heard about, or even problems that theoretically might happen.

Did you include?

A) Bad call by a referee,
B) Missing a move,
C) Out of bounds,
D) Slip throw,
E) Conditioning questions,
F) Falling behind early in the match.

What did you say in each situation? Write what you remember saying the last time this happened to you.

What should you think? Write down what you think is best for you to say to yourself in these situations.

What do you want to think? Now decide what you are going to say in each of these situations.

More on your perfect match

Let's look farther into your perfect match. There are several ways to look at a perfect match plan. A few pages back we asked you to design a perfect match. You probably wrote down a quick pin for yourself or either you wrote that you stomped your opponent. Yes, you're right, that would be a great match, but I am looking for more than that.

I want you to think about how you would win a hard fought 3-2, or 3-1 overtime match. Why? By planning situations ahead of time we have something to call upon when the time comes. We can actually build mental responses to events before they occur. Now, that might sound strange, but isn't that what we do in our technique practice? We build a physical response to an anticipated position!

So, now, write down the thoughts you would like to have for each portion of a tough match. Explain the situation, and then tell what you think you should be thinking. Write the statement or idea just as you would think it. Use the words that you actually want to say during your competition. If it's rough talk, so be it. This is your personal statement, so make it in your words (Believe me when I say that several of our athletes have colorful expressions for their self-talk statements. If that is the way you think, then write it down!)

Write the thoughts you want to have:
Right before the match:

Walking onto the mat:

First contact:

First series:

Takedown focus:

Motion:

Top (par tarre) offense:

Bottom (par tarre) defense:

Second series:

Opponent's flurry:

Bad call:

"I want to get into overtime. I know I have trained harder than anyone and I have my plan ready. I'll bang his head, brawl and beat him until he steps back."
World Champ Dennis Hall, entering any overtime.

Evaluating your plan

(Your match versus the information we have)

The next step on the road to your perfect match is for you to look at the things you have already written. As you reread the information decide if it fits in with what you really need. The plan is for you, but you will be evaluating your program to see if it agrees with what the nation's most successful athletes are doing. If it is, then congratulations, you are doing fine. If it is not, then you will need to reconsider your approach and make any needed changes.

How does one evaluate his plans and strategies? By comparing his plans with successful wrestlers' and coaches' strategies and ideas. Look at what they are doing successfully and try to imitate what will help you.

Your questions

What are the trends in our sport. How do the elite athletes score against other elite wrestlers? How are most matches won? Are there differences between high school, college and open matches? What about the perfect Greco match? We want you to look at your approach to your matches and then compare it to what is happening in your style and level of wrestling.

How close is your model to your coach's model? Do you follow your weight class' trends? Do you understand what other athletes are trying and why? If you are comfortable with your match and your coaches have been over your plan, then anchor it to your mind and make it automatic. If you see conflicts between what you do and what has been being successful, then ask one of the coaches to talk to you about it. You are the man. You have to perform. I want you to be confident in what you do.

The model

Our sport is always changing. The rules, the length of the matches, the types and physical makeup of the

athletes are all aspects that may change, and this leads
to possible problems. Some of our older athletes grew
up under a different set of rules and ideas. They know
the old sport, but new rules and new strategies have
produced major changes in how we need to look at match
strategies.

Even with the changes in wrestling we can still identify
several ideas that are constant in the sport. These ideas
should be incorporated in any athletes perfect match
plans. Take a moment to think about these ideas and
then see how they fit into your plans.

1) Basic skills are still vital. Good stance and motion
have to be included in your plans. An athlete who is just
standing there looks passive and becomes an easier
target for his foe. Work to gain good position, then
maintain it throughout the battle. Stance, position,
motion, and level changes are as important as ever.
(USA Wrestling promotes the "basic skills" approach.
Check into that to see if you are working on building a
good base for your techniques by using the basic skills.)

2) On your feet, low risk, high percentage moves seem
to be the thing to do. Does your strategy and technique
selection fit this approach? Are you trying fancy moves
that are dangerous? Do you have a safe series that will
work in a close match? Do you have a series you can use:
when you are in the lead? late in a match? against a
tough opponent?

3) Don't just *let* passivities or stalling calls happen.
Force them. Cause them. Make them happen. Include
this as part of your strategy. Develop specific series that
make it look like you are busting your butt to score! <u>Get
that point in scholastic. Get the man on the mat in
Freestyle and Greco.</u> (This becomes very important in
elite Greco-Roman. We are seeing more putdowns than
takedowns. Don't be left out! If you are having trouble
with the takedown, you might want to actively shift gears
to focus on the putdown. Try to get a passivity call.)

4) Focus on bottom defense. Develop a defensive dialogue that makes you think "stay active on bottom", or encourages you to score. Refuse to lose on bottom! Stop his offense by being determined and focused. In scholastic think, "Hand control, motion! Get out. Plant my foot, explode, score. Escape!" These types of thoughts will be a key to your successes.

Coaches concepts

Conditioning is another key. Learn to pace. This means to attack with intensity, and then actively recover while holding good position. You can think of this as pulsing. Stance and position should be a focus. Remember to focus on a good selection of moves. Does your approach fit the research model or your coach's model?

Use the mat! Know where you are and act accordingly. Keep your back to the center. Shoot through the zone. Make the official decide if your foe is stalling, was pushed, or if he is fleeing. Keep your patience. If you are in better shape, it will show in the matches if you keep your head.

If your match strategy does not include these thoughts, then justify to yourself why. If it is working, then you can continue, but if you are having problems, identify what is wrong and work to improve or correct that issue.

A quick method to analyze

Select a specific situation that occurs in a match, and then write your dialogue.

Example: *I am ahead late in the match.*

What do you want to think?

"Move to a plan B series where I attack with safe, outside motion moves. Duckunder or arm drag series. Motion, look like I'm trying to score. Short arms, elbows in. Don't reach or give a big move. Motion. Action. Duck, duck, duck! Good position. Good stance. Keep after him. Drill him. Spank him. Score off this safe series."

Ask yourself- "What do the most successful athletes do in this situation?"

Is there a difference between what you do and what they do?

Why?

If there is a difference in what you do and what the top guys are trying, then figure out why and what you need to do. Are you successful with what you are doing? Can you take your performances to the next level doing what you are doing? If not, then change.

Next, think about another situation. (You can think about many different things-- what you are doing on bottom, where your head goes on a single, what setups you use for each specific move, how you counter a certain move.) Use the same evaluation--What is the situation? What do you do? What do the elite do? Are you in line with their approach? If not, then why? Accept what you are doing is right, or change your approach.

Matt Ghaffari says his mental skills program contributed to his successes. Here he displays the Silver medal he won at Atlanta's Olympic Games.

photo courtesy of Matt Ghaffari

Kendall hits a big move on 1995 World champion Terry Brands in one of their matches that decided who represented the US at the 1996 Olympics. Many experts feel this series actually decided the Olympic champion.

Photo by Kim Gabrielson
Courtesy of Kendall Cross

Section III Psychological Issues

1) Stress
2) Physical or mental
3) Focus
4) Activation
5) Centering
6) Flow
7) Morphing
8) Affirmations

Let's step away from the idea of perfect matches for a moment and focus on some skills that can help you control your mental state. These techniques may sound a little funny, or touchie-feelie, but they are effective.

Not every one of these ideas will work for you, since every athlete is different. Read about each and decide how it fits your thinking and personality style. If it fits, then use it. If not, then throw the idea away.

Remember, we are playing a game when we wrestle. It is not real life, so we can do some silly things to help us. The ultimate goal as an athlete is to be so well trained that you don't think, you just perform. You become childlike and have a good time.

You may already have noticed that several of our ideas are encouraging you to become more childlike in your approach. That's because kids usually play up to their potential in backyard games. They focus on the process and get into the game, hardly ever worrying about the outcome.

Kids make believe. Sometimes they act as if they are someone else. They experiment and try new things. That is the way we want to become. Focus on doing your thing. Stop thinking about: What if this happens? What if I lose? What if I can't do it? What will so and so think?

Get in gear. Do as you have trained and have a good time being successful.

Stress

Stress can be a friend or foe. Too little stress and you will be under-aroused and not be motivated to perform. Too much stress and you will be over-aroused and may panic or freak-out, thereby harming your performance. Either way, your wrestling suffers.

From my work with elite athletes, I would have to say that over-activation (too much stress) is the major problem that athletes mention. That makes sense. You are performing. You see every match as a challenge. This offers many opportunities for stress to develop, and often this stress becomes too much.

Where does stress come from?

You! Yes, it is produced by you, so you control it. Now, that may sound a little strange. You know that you sometimes experience pressure and it is caused by many different things: money, love life, having to make the team--all kinds of things! But, when psychologists research stress and pressure, they find some interesting results. Some people are bothered by certain things, while other people have no problem with the same situations. After studying this, the experts have come up with the answer.

> <u>Nothing</u> in particular causes stress. Stress is caused by <u>how you</u> perceive an idea, requirement or expectation. It is really in how the individual interprets the events or situations.

So?

So, any stress you feel will be caused by how you are looking at the situation. It is coming from your picture of how things *should* be, and what you think *needs* to be. By placing such values on an idea, you begin to produce tension, stress, anxiety, or pressure.

Another common problem is that we are always looking into the future, wondering about what will happen. We have no control over the future, so it can make us worry about the uncertainty. This builds stress. Now, couple this--should be, needs to be, oughta be, has to be--attitude with the uncertainty of the future, and you can see a great opportunity for us to produce too much stress.

What can a wrestler do if he feels too much stress?
1) Understand that you are making the stress.
2) Step back and identify what you are stressing over.
3) Look for the solution to that specific problem. (What do I want to do about it?)
4) Get to work on the solution.
5) If there is not immediate solution, then tell yourself to let go.
6) Refocus on an idea or thought that will help you.

By understanding that you are in control, you are a step closer to actually being in control. You have the power, so use it!

A simple trick you can try is to reframe the stress. Call it *excitement* instead of nervousness. Often times it is excitement that you are labeling as nervous tension. The only difference between excitement and nervousness that I can get my athletes to explain is in the athlete's perception of the outcome. If the athlete is worried about poor performance, he labels it nervousness. If there is positive thinking going on, then the feeling is noticed as excitement. Who controls that process? The athlete! So, if the athletes can control or direct their thinking, they can help themselves with the concept of nervousness. Try this approach. Tell yourself that you are excited and you are going to do well! It helps.

Stress: Is yours physical or mental?

Stress affects wrestlers in different ways. Some sense a nervousness in their body. They feel "uptight", "tense", or "frozen". Others notice negative talk floating into their thinking. They can't shake these ideas of worry or dread. The bad news is that both of these types of stress can negatively affect your performances. Each can eat at you, causing you to shift your focus from completing the task, to focusing on the problem. But there is some good news. There are methods we can employ that will help to calm or control both types.

Somatic (body) stress is when you react physically to a situation. Your body becomes tense. A diagram of this type of stress shows the body reacting first, triggering anxiety, and poor performances.

Bodily Stress--> Anxiety--> Performance Problems

The most common and easiest method of arresting the development of this physical tension is the use of deep breathing, or relaxation methods. (An example of a relaxation script is included later on page 93.)

With *cognitive stress* (negative thinking) the wrestler builds anxiety by thinking negatively about an event or task. These thoughts then cause physical symptoms that may interfere with an athlete's performance. The goal to stopping this type of nervousness is to stop the negative thoughts, and then move on to positive or neutral thinking. It sounds easy, but it can be hard to train yourself to stop, and refocus. A diagram of this type of stress would show negative thoughts occurring first, followed by bodily stress which could interfere with performance.

Negative thoughts-->Bodily Stress-->Performance Problems

Somatic Stress

If your <u>body</u> shows signs of stress first, control your physical symptoms by relaxing. A short version of a relaxation script may be all you need. Shift right into the script if you feel your body begin to tighten up. Some programs suggest that you use this relaxation system before you enter any type of stressful situation. Calm yourself before you begin to feel tense. Make yourself relax. Train yourself to go through a quick edition of your favorite relaxation script anytime you foresee a tense situation. Use the relaxation to prepare yourself to enter the setting.

How do you use these techniques? It is easy. When you think you are entering a stressful situation, recognize the fact, and then take a moment to gain control by starting your stress reduction techniques. You are in control. Learn to assert yourself. Take control of your body's reactions. Develop a short personal script that you can use. Say something like: *"Okay, I'm starting to feel a little tense. I need to get control. Slow down. Take a breathe. Relax. Think about _____ (something you think is relaxing). Now, that's better!"*

The key is to understand that you can control your stress. By employing a stress reduction technique before the anxiety takes control, you win the battle without having to fight. You can also use your stress control as you leave a stressful situation. This will help you relax and be able to transfer into your next activity without suffering from any lingering anxiety.

Negative Thoughts

Wrestlers whose thoughts wander to negative ideas can apply a negative-thought-stopping strategy to control their problem. This stops the stress from taking the next step and affecting your body. First identify the negative thoughts, and then redirect your thinking to what you want to be doing. Get into the present and do what you need to do instead of focusing on worries or negative concerns.

Most athletes tell me they feel stressed-out when their minds focus on negative thoughts or ideas. "I can't." "I'll never." "I don't think..." These are NEGATIVE SELF-TALK STATEMENTS and they work against good performances and fun. Basically, any thinking or talking that moves you away from your goal is bad, and you must correct or redirect this thinking by completing three steps.

1) Realize it. Identify negative self-talk. Remember, it is any thinking that focuses on worry, doubt, or failure. Recognize any negative thoughts that may be entering your thinking, and then admit that you are negative talking--that you are negging out and starting to defeat yourself. Once you identify the negative thoughts, you can start to take corrective measures.

2) Stop it! Stop the negative. Make yourself stop. Say "I am being negative--I've got to stop. It will not help. It will only hurt if I keep thinking this way." It sounds easy, but it takes an effort to stop this process. Some folks suggest that you say "STOP!" aloud to trigger or cue yourself to change the behavior. This will give you a moment to collect yourself.

3) Redirect your thoughts. If you just say "stop", chances are that you will return right back to your previous thinking, and your tension will continue to build. Learn to self-talk yourself into positive or neutral thinking. Think: "What should I be focusing on right now?" "What can I be doing that will help me?" "What should I be doing right now?" Come up with an answer, and then shift to that task and get back into the groove. If you can't think of anything, just shift your thoughts to your task and get going.

Closing

So, learn which type of stress affects you the most. Are you physically stressed, or are you thinking too much? After you have identified your specific style of stressing, practice the proper controlling methods. It won't be hard; it will just take a little time and patience.

After you begin to feel confident with the methods, you will be able to apply them in real situations. The key is to recognize the stress as it begins to build, decide what type it is, then shift into your control strategy. That sounds pretty easy, and it actually is.

Focus

One of the basic ideas behind stress control is that of controlling one's focus. When we look at stress and identify its components and causes, we can actually see that much of our stress is caused by inappropriate focus. Often, you are thinking about things that are not helping the situation. You focus on the wrong things, and these things cause you to spend extra energy on worry!

What is focus? Focus is the ability to concentrate on a specific area or idea. It allows us to function in a complicated environment. Without focus we would be overloaded with too much input from our senses. Finding the appropriate item or activity to focus on can become hard. Problems occur when we focus on things that are not important, or when we fail to focus on the important ideas.

Where can we focus? There are lots of things we can focus on. It is funny that we often hear coaches telling their athletes to "focus". Their athletes are focused. We are always focused! We may not be focused on the appropriate topic or activity, but we are focused!

Where should we focus? On tasks that will allow us to achieve our goals or solutions to problems. Focusing on worries, negative thoughts, or problems will not help. Negative focus freezes us and keeps our attention glued to the problem. That leaves no room for thinking of corrections or improvements.

Framing and reframing are the concepts that we respond to things based upon how we look at the idea. How you frame a thought will set the stage for how it affects you.

Kurt Angle's example

Kurt had a stellar year in 1995. He won a national championship in Las Vegas, and then captured the World championship in Atlanta. Yet Kurt had a concern. His "on top" or par terre techniques weren't working to his satisfaction. Kurt was training hard to become the next

100 kg Freestyle Olympic Champion, but he felt he had to improve on top to be in the hunt.

"I was weak in par terre top--I knew that if I became good--just one or two solid turns, that I would win the Olympics. At the worlds I had no turns. At the Olympics I had five turns. I did change my practice focus from 80% feet and 20% top/bottom, to 50% feet--50% par tarre. I focused on my gut wrench and leg lace."

Kurt did an outstanding job of changing his focus. He evaluated where he was and what he needed to do, and then focused on changing what he felt needed changing. He worked more on his top techniques, bringing them up to the level of his takedown and defensive abilities.

Did it pay off? You decide!

Olympic Champion Kurt Angle changed his focus in practice so he could improve his top techniques. Here he shows the results of his training by turning his Olympic opponent with a tough gut wrench.

photo by Doug Reese

Activation

Getting ready to compete is an important part of the competition, yet many people take it for granted. Why warm-up? Why does coach make us be quiet before our games? Why am I always so nervous? These types of questions are based upon the idea of activation--getting physically and mentally at the right level to perform. But activation is more than just getting fired up; as a matter of fact, you can get too fired up. And being either too hot or too cold can negatively affect a performance.

Goldilocks and the three bears
We use the terms *activated* and *aroused* when we discuss how excited a player is. Performance theory suggests that an athlete has an optimum or best level of excitement. Too relaxed or "cold", and the performance levels dip. Too nervous or "hot", and the athletes become overloaded with worries. Either way, an athlete can loose focus and the performance may suffer.

The easiest way to explain this concept is to use the story of Goldilocks. You know the story of Ms. Goldilocks. She was always having trouble with things being too much, too little--too hot, too cold. She was forever hunting the situation that was just right. This can be a problem for athletes of all ages and levels. Just like Goldi and her porridge, athletes must find a point where their arousal is just right-- they must learn to make sure that their mental porridge is 'just right'.

Too cold?
Picture yourself in a deep sleep. Would you be able to perform well? Probably not. You would be slow to react, and your decision-making system would not be in full force. This often happens to athletes. Some have been over-confident and not focused on the task at hand. Others may have been thinking about another topic and forgot to warm up. Either way, their performance could suffer.

An athlete may encounter this under-arousal in several types of situations. Early morning matches are often difficult to prepare for. Preliminary matches against unseeded athletes can also present arousal problems. These situations may cause an athlete to fail to prepare. By failing to prepare their minds and bodies for the competition, the athlete doesn't move well, is uptight, and probably more prone to injury. Often under-activated athletes look like they are in a daze, and they appear uninspired.

Individual sports place the burden of getting aroused on the athlete. These sports have the athletes participating at different times during the day. The athletes tend to be left to their own to warm-up. The athlete has the normal pressures of competition, and the added problem of deciding what will be the best method to prepare his body for competition. Older or more experienced athletes may have developed a ritual or routine, but the younger athletes often have trouble with this added burden.

Too hot!
What about being too hot? Picture yourself getting so excited that you have a heart attack. Could you perform? Probably not. Yet, many athletes put themselves in this position by focusing on things they can't control or by worrying about topics that are inappropriate. Athletes talk themselves into anxieties by looking at their competition, comparing won/loss records, or even judging a foe's ability by the tradition of the opponent's school. This would make the athlete's mental porridge too hot! The athlete becomes too nervous and would begin to focus on the stress, not the performance.

So, being too nervous or too calm can actually harm performances. To be at your best, you must learn to control arousal and keep the excitement at a level that is "just right" for your optimal performance.

Sounds Easy!

Yes, that sounds easy--control your activation and keep it to a certain level. Nothing hard about that. Unfortunately, that probably is one of our athlete's biggest mistakes--thinking that activation is automatic. You can control your arousal, but it is not that easy. Let's think for a moment. What actually happens in the world of athletics? What happens to you? Too hot? Too cold? What do you need?

So what do you really need to know about arousal and activation?

Keep these simple ideas in mind.

1. There is a certain level of arousal that you will need to reach to be ready for your performance.
2. This level is different for each athlete.
3. You may have to prepare yourself. Coach may be tied up.
4. "Too cold", and you will be flat, or sluggish
5. "Too hot", and you will be overexcited, jumpy and may lose some technique or even fail to shoot.
6. You can learn to adjust your levels by controlling your mental skills and directing your focus and self-talk.

Athletes who want to become more activated should do more physical warmups. Jump up and down. Slap your thighs. Run several short windsprints. Get excited.

Wrestlers who want to de-activate (bring themselves down a notch) would practice stress control methods such as:

1) Take a slow and deep breath.
2) Wiggle your fingers and hands while blowing out your breath.
3) Tell yourself to relax or focus.
4) Visualize yourself successfully completing a move or technique, or even see yourself on the victory stand.
5) Smile and enjoy our sport!

Centering

What is it? **Centering** is a focus/refocusing technique that allows athletes to recover composure and to redirect focus by taking a breath and focusing on the act. It is promoted as a basic stress-control technique.

Idea behind the method
Sport psychologists tell us that it is important for the athlete to "stay in the present". We can't control the future, nor the past, so thinking about these time frames can cause anxiety and stress. Yet, many athletes place themselves in the past by dwelling on what has happened. Others jump to the future to worry about what might occur. Both of these situations can negatively affect performances.

Centering helps you to 'stay in the present' by helping you concentrate on your body and your breathing. This allows you to focus on things other than the stress, bad calls, what happened, or what will happen on the mat. The mere act of thinking about your breathing changes your focus from the negative or anxiety causing events, to the present task. This kicks out the negative and helps you regroup your thoughts.

How do I center?
Focus on breathing a slow, steady stream of air in through your nose. Feel the air enter your lungs and settle into the center of your body. Blow out through your mouth while thinking a key word or phrase that helps you to refocus on what you need to be doing. Some athletes choose to think, "What do I need to do now?" Others say, "Center". Some even close their eyes and envision a successful move. You can develop your own key word or phrase. Just make it one that has meaning to you.

How do I learn the skill?

Centering can become automatic if you practice it enough. *Center* yourself after flurries in practice. Teach yourself to use every break to regain focus by *centering*. Train yourself to control your thinking by using this centering skill as your cue. Invoke that automatic refocus.

When do I apply this skill?

Center any time you have a pause in action. Simply take your breath and repeat your key word to refocus on your goals. When *centering* becomes automatic, you will be almost 'machine-like' in your response to match situations.

What will it do for me?

Once you learn this skill, you will notice a definite change in the thinking patterns you use in your matches. You will spend less time thinking about problems and more time focusing on solutions. You will have less stress, and you will enjoy more success.

So, you make the call. Is it something that will benefit you in your matches? If so, then <u>practice it daily</u> until you master the skill. It is a simple and effective way for you to control of your performance self-talk and focus.

Example:

A flurry takes you out of bounds late in the third period. The score is close. Take a deep breath and notice the air go into your body. Feel it refresh you and give you energy. Think: *"What do I need to do now?"* Then come up with a specific plan. Get into your position with that thought in mind. If you are on bottom, think bottom task thoughts with affirmations. *"I'm going to explode up. Hand control, weight back into him. Explode, quick, coming up. Nothing can stop me!"*

Flow

Psychologists call it "the holistic sensation people feel when they are totally involved, or in automatic pilot." Michael Jordan says, "Man, I was in my zone."

No matter what it is called, *flow* is the perception that we have when our ability level equals our challenges. It is when we get so involved with our match that we actually get lost in the event. We lose the awareness of time. (It may slow down or speed up!) You know what you are doing, but you have no thoughts of trying to make yourself perform. There is a great sense of control. You enjoy moments of effortless motion. You perceive things almost as if they were a great dream. No worry of winning or losing; you are just part of the match.

When we talk to successful athletes, we find that many of them are consistently able to reach such a state and that it tends to help them achieve great performances. By reaching flow, or getting into their zone, these athletes perform at a level beyond that of normal expectations. Most of us can remember such a moment if we try. And it is usually a match or moment of great performances.

So, how can one reach this state of flow?

There is no one certain way. Flow occurs when you have set the table by doing all of the right things. And these things are:

1) Frame the match in a positive light. "This is what I like doing. I like to wrestle. No, I <u>love</u> wrestling and it is time!" Nothing is going to stop a man *living his dream*.

2) Learn to capture that feeling of nervous excitement. Be a little on edge, but in control. Reframe the word "nervous". Call it "excited". Look forward to the competition.

3) Keep a narrow focus on what you want to do. Constantly wipe away any negative or outside thoughts that might interfere with your match.

4) Remind yourself of your level of preparedness. You

are physically ready. You are a great athlete who is properly trained. Use your affirmations to put you into an   almost trance-like state.

5) Return to a moment when everything was going your way. Remember where it was and how it felt. Capture that feeling. Take it into your match with you.

6) Let go. Wrestle like you do when you are enjoying our sport the most.

Factors that prevent or disrupt flow

1) Physical problems or mistakes. (Injuries, mistakes, or fatigue can enter into your thinking and cause you to think about problems.)

2) Poor   focus.   (Distractions,   surprises,   and interruptions may bring you out of a flow state.)

3) Negative attitude. (Negative self-talk, and doubt cause you to move away from just enjoying the process. Negative thinking is the opposite of what you are searching for.)

Flow doesn't just happen. Your mental and physical state, and the things that happen around you interact to influence its appearance. So, train yourself to set the stage, then hit the mat with a confident game plan. Anticipate the match in a positive light. Want to be there. Plan on doing well.

Then let go. Do it. Have fun. The more joy and happiness you can find in wrestling, the better off you will be and the more often you will be able to find that flow state.

(Thanks to Weinberg and Gould for their ideas on flow and the flow state in *Foundations of Sport and Exercise Psychology*, 1995.)

Morphing

Grant me the power to change what I can

When you were a kid did you ever imagine you were someone else? Have you ever seen a young basketball player say, "I'm Michael Jordan! Watch me pop this net!"? Imagining that they are some superhero or superstar is a normal game among youngsters. It offers the child a chance to be creative and to explore new situations. Unfortunately, as we grow older we are often discouraged from being childlike. Our parents or other adult figures tell us to quit imagining things--to grow up and be an adult.

Change!

But you still have that skill that you used as a child. You can still change or *morph* into anyone or anything you want. (Then you can use their special talents to help you in your practices or in your matches.)

Why?

Morphing can do several things.

1) It allows athletes to remove themselves from pressure situations by "becoming someone else".

2) It allows them to try different styles by "using another person's technique".

3) It gives them a "mental game" to play.

4) It puts "fun" back into practices and matches.

But into whom or what?

There are several ways to change. Some people like to change into animals. Others like to change into their heroes, or World champions in their weight. Still others turn into cartoon or make-believe figures.

Suggestions? Who is better in par tarre defense than World Champions Dennis Hall (Greco), or Kevin Jackson (FS)? Could you duplicate their styles? Who is known for their tremendous low-angle attacks? Turn into John Smith and bite those ankles. Who do you admire for their top or par tarre offense? Or how about swelling up to double your size? Imagine turning into a 300 pound person and gluing your hips to the mat. Who could turn you? What if you turned into the Hulk, and then grabbed that gut wrench or shot that half-nelson?

How?

Tell yourself you want to be that person, and then duplicate their style and techniques, or their size or super strength. Don't analyze their methods; just fight like you think they would fight. Focus on becoming them and being successful at your task.

So,

Do it! Change. Make yourself be someone or something else. You will be surprised at the outcome. You will have fun and enjoy it while picking up some extra techniques or methods.

Yes, it sounds weird when you first think about the skill, but many athletes employ this method. They use it for practice and for stressful situations. So, give it a try. It could help you relax a little and maybe assist you in reaching that next step on your road to success. At the very least it will help you bring a little fun back into the practice room.

Side story

I was working with an African Olympic runner. One day we were talking about fighting through the pain of a 5000 meter race. Edith told me about one of her idols. "I wish I could fight like her. She fights so very hard."

I asked Edith why she couldn't turn into that girl? Edith laughed a little nervous laugh, and we talked about the idea for a while, and then let it drop.

Two weeks later Edith came back and excitedly told me about a race. "Coach, it worked. I changed into her at two and a half miles and ran great. I cut almost twenty seconds off my time. Because I was her, I could not hurt! I was able to fight and run harder to the finish."

Affirmations explained

Confidence plays an important part in what and how you do. If you are not confident or if you are shakey, then you can have problems with your performances. To be the best at what you want to be, you must believe that you are the best!

USA Wrestling's National Greco Coach Steve Fraser says we must be *fanatical*, and he is right. The day of the casual amateur coming in and winning in our sport is long gone. This fact demands that we must make wrestling important in our life if we want to reach a higher level of achievement. To be a champion, we must think we are champions. We must believe in our ability and use this belief to fuel our confidence.

So, how do we develop and keep that "best in the world" attitude? Many sports psychologists suggest that elite athletes begin a program of affirmations. Kay Porter and Judy Foster promote the idea of affirmations in their book *The Mental Athlete*. They say that "positive self-statements are a powerful weapon we can use to combat the destructive self-beliefs and talk we confront from time to time during work-outs, and, more specifically, during competitions." "Affirmations will short circuit the negative talk."

Wrestlers can compile a series of "I am" statements that help them focus on their skills in the different areas of competition. These statements are reminders of what the athlete is and what he realistically can do.

I am statements
You may think that making I am statements can be a little embarrassing. Saying, "I am the best in the state", when in actuality, you have only finished second before this year may be hard for you to believe. That's okay. Your brain will learn to believe and your body will just follow suit. Your body is a robot and does not judge, so get to work training it.

Where would you start? That's easy, start with true ideas that you can readily accept. Then, as you become comfortable with the concept, start using statements that you think you are close to reaching.

Most experts suggest that the athletes make statements that are in the present. By saying "I am....." you tell yourself that you have already achieved this goal. If you tell yourself "I will be the best" it places the statement into the future and leaves room for doubt. Some athletes prefer to say "I will", and if that works for them, then it is okay, but "will" shows the future, and the future never gets here. For that reason, I usually use "I am" statements when I help an athlete build an affirmation tape.

Many of my elite athletes use this method to prepare for competition. They have their list, and some even have tapes of their statements.

"I looked at my affirmation list every night before I went to bed. To be the best in the world you must think you are the best in the world, and I taught myself to believe that," says Dennis Hall. *"I am in the best shape. I am going to pummel his head. I am going to wear him down. I know that, say that and believe that, and it becomes true."*

Applying the technique

At first you may not feel comfortable. You may have some question about the truth of the statements. That's okay. I also use this system to find out where my athletes are <u>not</u> confident, and then we work on improving that area. Say what? Okay. Let's say when we talk, you say that being in top shape is important for you to be a winner. If you don't include that in your affirmations, I would ask you why you left it out. If you are not comfortable saying "I am in great shape", then by working together, we will either get you into great shape so you can honestly say the affirmation, or you will learn to believe in yourself by focusing on other affirmations.

Section IV Your perfect warm-up

1) Rituals for preparation
2) A perfect warm-up
3) Your perfect warmup

"I was having trouble with my prematch preparation until I made my warmup into a ritual. I started doing everything the same. I noticed that I felt ready for my matches." **Dennis Hall, Greco-Roman Olympic Silver Medalist**

"Self-talk is extremely important during your warm-up period. I constantly tell myself that I will win. Over and over, I say ' Kendall, you will win! Kendall, you will Win!' When it is a high pressure match, I tell myself that the match is no big deal. The reason I do this is to take pressure off myself. I constantly reassure myself that no matter what happens out there, the result will not, by any means, shake up the cosmos. This relieves me of my anxiety. An athlete tends to relax both physically and emotionally when the pressure is off. The most comforting self-talk before matches is the kind that reassures you of your preparation. If you have trained hard and trained smart, you will be able to tell yourself you are READY! You can say to yourself 'I have done my homework! I'm totally prepared!' This is a boost like no other. There's a catch to this approach. You must train hard and train smart. Being prepared mentally and physically is omnipotent."

"Also of great importance is the ability to block out negative thoughts. Negative thoughts will, like weeds in a garden, strangle the positive thoughts. Bombard your mind with positive thoughts. This positive thinking will, in turn, strangle the negative thoughts." **Kendall Cross, 1996 Olympic Gold Medalist**

Rituals for preparation

Warming up

Most athletes accept the idea of warming up. A warmup allows the body to activate and become aroused. It lubricates joints, stretches muscles, and helps the athlete become physically prepared. But many athletes warmup in a haphazard way. A time that should be a period of getting into optimum readiness for competition can become a moment of lost opportunities, or even worse--a time of too much stress and anxiety.

Order from chaos

Warming-up can also offer time for planning your strategies and tactics or even controlling your stress. During your warmup you can accomplish many things that will help you in your performance, but how can you be sure that you warm up properly and cover all of your needed concerns? By developing a ritual, or specific way of doing things. We all have special ways of doing things. By organizing and following through with your special procedure, you develop a comforting system of preparing for competition.

So, what do you need?

It is easy. You just need to get things organized in a comfortable sequence. What do you like to do to get ready? Think about it, and then repeat the same routine every time. Use your ritual to *transform* from anxiously awaiting your match, to being well prepared and ready to go. You could say this is the time that an athlete goes from being a spectator to being a participant. How do you make this transformation? What do you need to do to be at your optimum level?

Design your ritual

Take a moment to decide what you like to do. Get it in your mind what you want to do and when. Lay out a step by step plan. Write it down if you like, and then practice it. Explain it to someone; let them read it over. Listen to it on tape. Repetition will help you "learn" how to prepare for competition. Learn it so well that you don't even think about it.

Your ritual is your friend

Get lost in your preparation. Everything is automatic as you go from step to step--no outside worries or cares. Just focus on your goals and get your mind and body ready. By entering your ritual, you retreat to a comfortable place--one you are familiar with. No matter where you are, you can now enter this 'place' where you feel good and know what is happening. Use your ritual to cue yourself to get into your zone.

Ritualized warmup

You might think, *"I'll do my stretches. That always helps. I feel good when I stretch, especially my lower back. That gets me ready to move. Five minutes stretching and then I'll jump my rope. Shoulders, back, neck, three, four, five. Getting ready to move."* Pick up your rope. *"Now, go! Jump, warming up good. Getting ready. I'll be ready. When I get warm I'm ready to go. Jump, two, three. Next I'll pummel, drill. I like that. Helps me to be ready. Gets me going. Stance, level, shoot. Great. I feel good. I am ready. Keep moving. Go."*

Learn to cruise through your standard warm-up, feeling good, thinking positive or task-based self-talk. Find your zone. Get into flow. You the man! Show it.

Close

There are many things an athlete can do to help control stress and to prepare himself for competition. The development of a prematch ritual is one of these things. Take some time to decide what you need, design yourself a definite ritual, and then use it. By ritualizing your prematch tasks, you help yourself shift into automatic, you become comfortable with where you are, and you stop worrying about unneeded concerns.

Individual plan for preparation

We have presented information based upon the questions athletes have asked during camps and interviews. We have completed several activities based on these ideas, explored new concepts, and focused on topics that wrestlers have told me were important to them. So, you have now been exposed to several ideas that should help with your understanding of mental skills. Our next step is to personalize the program so that it meets your specific needs.

Your plan

I asked you to think about what you wanted to do and what you needed. Let's take the mental skills ideas that we have looked into and then customize them for you. After all, you know more about yourself than anyone else. You are the expert. So, take a moment and record what you need and what you want to do.

1) How do you get ready for a match?
Describe your prematch focus and preparation. (Do you have a RITUAL?)
It should be as detailed as possible. If you still don't really have a specific pattern or plan, describe what you usually do.

How long before your match do you start to get ready?

2) Your personal needs
Do you want someone to help you during your routine?
  If so, what kind of help do you want?
Do you want to know your opponent's tendencies? (A
  scouting report.)
Do you want to have positive encouragement?
Do you:
  a) want to talk to people, or
  b) have someone screen you from others?
Do you have a specific person who works best with you?
Anyone whom you would like to stay away from?

3) Pulling it together
Now go back to your prematch description. Use the
information from there and from your personal needs
section to design your perfect warmup. Write it. Be as
specific as possible.

Suggestion
Let your coaches know of anything you feel will assist
you in preparing for your competition.

Your perfect warm-up

Now list what you will do and what you will be thinking during each phase of your perfect warm-up. The more specific you are and the more information you write, the better your warm-up will be.

1) How will you warm-up? What will you do?

2) What will your first actions or activities be?

3) What will you do for the next five minutes?

4) What stretching will you do?

5) Any other activities?

Now, go back and <u>add the thoughts you would think</u> as you go through the first five steps.

What thoughts and ideas would you like to think about the upcoming match?

Good! Now you are ready to wrestle.

Kendall might have envisioned this, but of the thousands of fans in attendance at the Olympics, few thought they would see Kendall toss his opponent in the finals. Here he throws Giuvi Sissaouri of Canada to take an early and insurmountable lead in the gold medal match.

photo by Doug Reese

Section V   Seeing is believing

1) Relaxation, visualization and simulation
2) Visualization by Kendall
3) Sleep induction
4) Affirmations

Who visualizes?
Almost everyone has used the skill. Just think back to when you were a kid. Did you visualize then? Of course, and you probably still do on occasion. It is a natural and relaxing thing to do. But it is an automatic thing so we often have problems when we first try to use the skill in an organized fashion.

There are several of our top athletes who use organized visualization as part of their practice. Kendall is one, and he will explain his methods in later pages.

Your body is a robot.
I have been using relaxation, visualization and hypnosis for several years now, and their affect upon athletes is incredible. If an athlete believes he can do something, then half the battle is already won. That is basically what we do with these skills: we teach the athlete to believe in himself and to respond in certain ways to specific situations. Once the athlete learns this and believes, he gains tremendous confidence, and his body becomes a robot. It automatically responds to his thinking.

Believing
To be it, you must first see it.
You achieve, you must first believe.
Thinking of doubt will leave you out.
Realize, visualize, actualize.
Make your plan to be the man!
Questions are the treatment, solutions the cure.

Relaxation, visualization and simulation

Research points again and again to the fact that the most successful athletes visualize and even dream about successful competitions. Many people don't want to openly talk about the process because of some old and close-minded attitudes among the general population, but rest assured--the top people do it!

The funny thing about visualization is that everyone does it, has done it, and will do it. That is because it is a natural thing. As kids, we all engage in visualizing with make believe friends or play partners. It is considered an everyday thing, yet when we grow older we move away from 'such childish things'.

Relaxation is a method of enabling athletes to relax their bodies, remove stress, and to clear their minds so that they may control their thinking. Relaxation is based upon clearing your mind of outside thoughts and allowing your body to become calm. There are several methods, but progressive relaxation appears to be the most widely used and most widely accepted among our athletes.

Visualization is another commonly used technique. In visualization, the athlete sees what he wants to do. pictures himself being successful and in completing both moves and matches. Visualization is not really what we need to be using. A more detailed method called *imagery* would probably be more appropriate. In imagery we see, feel, hear, smell, and taste (if possible!) all of the parts of any vision.

Simulation takes the vision a step farther. In simulation, we encourage the athletes to see themselves in specific situations. They should imagine every detail possible, including noting their opponent, arena, and even the referee. I encourage the wrestler to be as specific as possible. For some, this technique takes repeated practice before it can be mastered. For others, it is a piece of cake!

Visualization by Kendall Cross

Kendall Cross, 1996 Olympic Gold Medalist, learned to use mental skills as an important part of his training. He visualized for many hours during the months leading up to the Nationals, Olympic Trials, and the 1996 Olympics. Kendall told me that by the time he had reached the Nationals and the Final Olympic Trials that he had visualized his "Perfect Matches" against specific opponents and knew exactly what he was going to do in each match!

On visualization

Kendall says, *"Visualization was extremely important in developing my confidence. Visualization increased my confidence to the point that I felt I could not lose. Your mind has trouble distinguishing between actual physical motion and mental imagery of that same motion. To the mind it is all the same. Therefore, it is effective to visualize yourself performing perfect techniques. It gives your mind a blueprint for those techniques. Granted you must practice them physically as well to develop the motor skills for that movement. Visualization is great because you can practice the art anytime. Before the 1996 Olympic trials, I used visualization every chance I could find. I used it at home while listening to my favorite music, while riding a stationary bike, sitting on an airplane, riding in a car, and just about any other time I could free my mind of distraction."*

"I'm sure you are asking: What did I see when I visualized? My visualization was multi-faceted. Not only did I visualize perfect technique, but I also saw the arena, the crowd, the referee...everything that goes along with the actual match. I would try to smell the gym, my opponent, popcorn at the concession stand, etc. The idea was to try to recruit my other senses to make it feel as real as possible. Obviously, I viewed myself wrestling, but I took it a few steps further. I would hear the crowd,

feel my opponent, and feel the mat. I would see myself on the winner's podium watching my flag go up as the Star-Spangled-Banner was being played. This was so much a part of my daily routine, that by the time I actually had to wrestle for the gold medal, I had been through it a thousand times. I had already won a gold medal over and over in my mind. Call it total preparation! Mind, body, and spirit in total synchronicity."

Kendall's Perfect Match

"I developed my perfect match by seeing myself using techniques that I most frequently use. These moves are my bread and butter techniques. I don't try to see myself throwing my opponent with a belly-to-belly supplex, because that is not realistic. I took my idea of a perfect match and wrote it down on paper. This was effective because I was able to go over it any time. I started my perfect match from the sounding whistle to getting my hand raised. It is a great advantage to have a plan for your matches. To see a match all the way through, before you ever actually wrestle the match is a powerful tool. I also made contingency plans, or different endings to my Perfect Match. This perfect match concept gave me a guide in which I could follow when it was time to make it a reality. During this process, I kept in mind that the match might not go as planned. I visualized dealing with setbacks and uncontrollable circumstances in a positive way. Bad calls, injuries, mistakes, and opponents' actions did not bother me due to my ability to focus on the task at hand."

Sleep induction

Many athletes tell me that they have trouble sleeping on the days before competitions. This is a normal thing that annoys a lot of athletes. We call this problem *insomnia*--the inability to achieve restful sleep. Fortunately, there are ways that you can learn to control this problem.

A weird fact is that often the athlete starts to worry about not sleeping. This, in turn keeps him awake. The actual worrying about worrying begins to compound and bring about the very problem he is trying to avoid!

What causes this problem? There are several complicated reasons, but as far as athletes are concerned the most common problem is overactive thinking. The athlete begins to focus on the future and "thinks" himself awake.

How does it affect athletes? The missed sleep reduces quality recovery time for athletes and also can leave a wrestler tired. Not sleeping compounds the physical tension and also allows the athlete to build a tremendous negative dialogue.

How can you overcome insomnia?

Trick your brain! There are some little mental tricks you can use that will help you get to sleep. Counting is a good one. Counting sheep or takedowns removes your line of thinking from the problem to a task.

The next idea is good for people who have been really tired and can remember that situation and feeling. We call this *anchoring*: when you have a specific feeling or thought about a past event.

Some of my athletes have had success in using a sleep tape we have made.

Script for sleep

Several of my athletes have experienced success with developing scripts that assists them in getting to sleep. Try this one. It is one I often use with my wrestlers.

First, lie down. Get comfortable. Loosen any tight clothing. Take a deep breath and then blow it out, slowly. Focus on feeling the air rush from your body. Feel the heat of the air as it takes away the stress and tension from deep with-in your body. Feel that heat in your throat. Feel your chest go up, and then follow it as it collapses, down, down, down into your body.

Good! Now focus on your body. Feel the weight of your body on the floor. Relax and let your body spread out like an ice cube on warm pavement. Search for the feeling. You can actually feel your body relax and spread out.

Next, locate the point where your spine touches the back of your head. Focus on that spot for a moment. Shut your eyes and allow that feeling to spread from the base of the neck to all parts of your neck, your back, and the rest of your body.

Feel the heaviness in your body. It feels as if the bed is lifting you up. Surrender to this feeling. Let go. Focus on your tiredness. Squeeze your eyelids together tightly and hold them there for a slow count to ten.

Now, with your eyes closed, look up and back into your head. You will feel your eyes looking up, as if they were looking under your scalp. As you look under your scalp, slowly count to fifteen, then relax. Let your eyes relax.

Take a deep breath. Blow it out. Tell your shoulders to relax. Let them sag under their own weight. Now allow your body to sink down into the bed. It is ready and wants to relax.

Good. Now focus on your legs. Make them heavy. Let them sink. Your feet will start to relax, and you will feel as if you are floating. Focus on that feeling, float on into a relaxed state, and allow your self to drift off to sleep. Think: *"sleepy, eyes heavy, body relaxed, resting."* Focus on the feeling this brings to your body and enjoy it. "Sleepy, eyes heavy, body relaxed, resting." Go to sleep, enjoy it, and awaken refreshed.

Affirmations to use

We said that affirmations are statements that give us self-confidence and allow us to believe in ourselves. Here is a list of affirmations that are used by some of our top athletes. Read them, select the ones you would like to use, and then incorporate them into your prematch ritual or your match dialogue. It may take some time to get used to saying the affirmations, but you can train yourself to believe by repeating the statements over and over.

You can also use these statement to identify areas that may be causing you some concern. Remember in our discussion on affirmations we talked about identifying problem areas. Read these affirmations to yourself and mark the ones you feel are not true for you. Decide if they need to be true for you to be successful. If they do need to be true, then decide how to make them true, and begin work on plans to improve those areas.

(Thanks to my clients who helped me assemble this list. Many of these affirmations were taken from Olympians' or All-Americans' perfect match dialogues.)

I am in better shape than anyone.
I am mentally tougher than anyone.
My endurance is unbelievable.
I can break everyone mentally.
I can push anyone around the mat.
I make people look passive.
I am the strongest wrestler in my weight.
I stay focused throughout my entire match.
I am the most talented athlete at this weight.
I am the most deserving.
I am the best prepared.
I want it the most.
I practice the right moves.
I am going to win.
I am feeling better than ever.

I am in the best shape of my life.
I am in the best environment possible for me.
I am confident.
I am sure.
I recover properly.
I have the best coaching.
I am eating right.
I am getting plenty of rest.
I am unbeatable.
I have great workouts.
I have great workout partners.
I have done the most work.
I have put in the most time.
I have sacrificed the most.
I am ready when I step on the mat.
I am strong.
My training is just right.
I am fast.
I am big.
I am the quickest.
I am mean.
I keep my cool, but apply constant pressure.
I have the courage and ability to conquer any fear.
I am ready for greatness and I will go for it.
I am determined.
I work hard and am smart.
I believe in myself and my abilities.
I have done this many times before.
I feel good.
I am the man.
I've got great offense.
I am an animal on top.
I can turn anyone.
I am a bad man on my feet.
I am going to kick butt.
I can stop anyone.
I've got great defense.
No one can turn me.
No one holds me down.
I have perfect defense.

I am tremendous on bottom.
I can score from bottom.
I plant my foot, explode up and escape.
I finish my shots.
I am focused when I step on the mat.
I keep good position.
I control our position on the mat.
I control the tempo.
I pressure my foe.
I battle.
I fight.
I win the flurries.
People fear me.
I know what to do.
It is time for me to look good!
I have a great _____. (Name your move.)
No one can stop my _____.
People fear my _____.
I can stop anyone's _____.
I can counter legs.
I take advantage of my opponent's mistakes.
I force my foe to make mistakes.
The longer the match goes, the tougher I am.
I love overtime, cause I kick booty.
I think clearly.
I have great strategy.
I know the rules.
I control my performance, so I perform well.

Now, write some of your own. (Write as many as you can.)
I
I
I
I
My
My
My
No one
   List at least thirty affirmations and repeat them daily.

Section VI   **Make it perfect**

1) Support groups
2) Competition
3) How would you lose?
4) Perfect match thoughts from the studs!
5) Solutions to problems
6) Your perfect match finalized
7) Match tape and relaxation script
8) Simulations (by Coach Doug Reese)
9) Post test
10) Closing

I worked with Matt Ghaffari for several years and watched as he solidified himself on the international level. He proved to be one of America's greatest Greco Heavyweights by placing in world competition, winning a World Cup title, and by capturing his Olympic silver medal. Matt took a different route to his successes than many of my other athletes. Matt likes to have a support group to help him with his training and competition, so, to his credit, he assembled an effective one.

Before the Olympics, Anatoly Petrosyan, USA's Greco-Roman resident coach jokingly said this about Matt, "Matt has many coaches. He has--ooh, around eight. He has diet coach, sport psychologist, weight coach, National coach, Olympic team coach, technique coach, mental skills coach, and me."

Matt said, *"I didn't want to have to think about every little thing. I would overload. So, I put together a group of experts that I trusted and I learned to work with them. Having people who are experts in their area to help you can mean a lot. I wanted them there and I used them."*

For some athletes this would be extreme, but for Mr. Ghaffari, this is what he felt he needed to perform at the top level, so this is what he used.

Support groups and support systems

We are affected by the events that go on around us. Is there any way we can lessen the negative and enhance the positive situations that we encounter?

Designing a support group

We all need certain things. Most of us have the ability to get these things if we have enough time and are not bothered with other important situations. Unfortunately, most of the time we can't take care of everything. So, we must learn to delegate authority and count on other people. Many athletes learn to organize and empower a partner or group to help them get through their competitions.

"My wife Crissy goes everywhere I go. She is an important part of my wrestling and I want her to be with me," explains Dennis Hall.

How does Matt Ghafarri use his support system? Matt says, *"I used my support group to keep me on track. We would make plans and discuss each person's role. Then everyone would pitch in."*

"My people would always remind me of things that would help. I learned the perfect warm-up and perfect match and followed that with the help of Coach Hendrix. My sport psychologist, Shawn, worked with me on a program and would also help me after weigh-ins. Randy Couture would talk to me during warm-ups and tell me things that he knew would help."

"I also used my family. I made sure to talk to my group throughout the year. I would get feedback and stay on track. By having a group in place and trusting them to do their job, I could stay in the right frame of mind and focus on my performance instead of worrying about other things. I felt more confident and I could stay on my program."

"By feeling confident, I could warm up, get ready and then I could go onto the mat and wrestle without worrying."

But, be careful. Often there are people around who will actually negatively affect your performances. You have to decide who is to be around, and who should go.

Systemized program

One suggestion we have discussed many times is the idea of ritualizing as much as we can. Get into a routine that help you get through your tasks. Set a time. Do things in the same order, every time. Teach your support group what you want and need.

Use your ritual. Do it over and over to ingrain it into your memory. Become happy with it and forget actively thinking about anything once you enter your space.

Scheduling vs. spur of the moment

Set your schedule based upon your personality type. Do you like your day planned minute by minute, or do you like to leave time for spur of the moment activities? Either way is okay--it all depends upon what you like and which makes you feel comfortable.

Some athletes like to stay busy because it takes their mind off upcoming bouts. Others like to take extra time to relax and recover.

Relaxing

If you have a favorite relaxation technique, then use it to allow your body to recover and your mind to clear. Many athletes tell me that by going through a self-guided relaxation they can rest better and recover faster. If you have trouble relaxing on your own, then get someone to help you make a tape or find someone to lead you through a session.

Research shows that positive talk is the best. Neutral or task-based thinking is next best. The worst by far is negative self-talk, and it must be controlled.

Remember our discussion on the two types of stress. If you have physical stress, then take a breath and go through a short physical relaxation. If it is overthinking you are fighting, then go into your negative-thought-stopping relaxation method.

Competition

There are many things an athlete can think about when it comes to preparing for a match. If not handled properly, any of these topics could cause problems with a performance. The key is to organize a system that is optimum. Consider what you need, what you like, and what is best for you, and then follow through on the plan. Stay away from negative influences. Focus on completing activities that are beneficial to you.

Three Phases of Preparation

I like to divide preparation into three phases:
1) build-up,
2) point of performance, and
3) competitive phase.

Each phase has a specific place in the mental skills program, and each phase can affect performance.

1) Build-up-- The build-up phase is the foundation for a good competition. It includes activities the day or two before your event. It is like setting the table. Narrow your focus from general life events to the competition. Begin to plan activities around your schedule for performing. Control as much as possible. Aspects of this phase include: last work-outs before the meet, eating, sleep or rest, your social activities, your focus, equipment or uniforms, and any other concerns that may affect your preparation.

2) Point of performance-- When athletes reach the gym they have different needs. Time management becomes a major concern. When do you perform? How much warmup do you need? Water? What is your focus? What are your game plans? Do you have your 'stuff' ready? Is your support group working? As you move closer to competition, activation and stress control become more important. Even things that appear to be minor can affect your performance if they are not taken care of.

3) Competition-- When your name is called, it is

SHOWTIME. Your thinking needs to shift from focusing on preparation to performing. Strategies and self-talk become important. Training and mental skills blend together. You compete, and then you receive feedback.

Now you should be ready to take a look into your system of preparation. Fill in the blanks, apply your needs to the following outline, and customize it to fit your personality. Then use the results to help prepare you for the big meets or tournaments that are headed your way!

Your Preparation Checklist

Build-up skills
1) Eating--What meals do you like to eat? How will you make weight? What will you eat the day before? The morning of? Is there anything you need to stay away from?
2) What work-out do you need the day before? How much stretching? Do you need to run the night before? How much exercise on the morning of competition?
3) What is your best rest or sleep schedule?
4) When do you organize your travel bag? What do you need to include?
5) What do you want to think about? Any visualization? Relaxation?
6) What types of social activities? Time alone? Someone to talk to?

Point of performance
1) What environment do you want in the stands?
2) How much warm-up? How much water?
3) What is your focus? Music? Rest? Relaxation?
4) How do you control your activation and stress?
5) What type of self-talk do you want to use?
6) Do you have a plan? An alternate plan (Plan B)?
7) What do you need from your support group?

Competition
1) What are your thoughts right before you compete?

2) Is your warm-up planned? Complete it.

3) Is your strategy planned for the match? Plan B?

4) What is your activation level? Need adjusting?

5) Did you visualize?

6) Scan your body. Make needed adjustments. Perform.

How to Prepare

So, how do you organize this total package of preparation? There are several things you can do to prepare.

1) You can't control the environment, but you can control your approach to performance. The greater the number of things you have organized, the closer you are to removing uncertainties which may cause stress.

2) Set a schedule. By knowing what you want to do and when, you remove questions that can affect your anxiety level.

3) Plan how to keep your schedule. Make alternate plans that can be used if a problem arises. Look at a worst case scenario and make a list of possible events. Be ready to handle each situation much like you practice to counter certain moves.

4) Ritualize. Develop a system or routine that is comfortable to you. Repeat it so much that it becomes automatic. Dress in the same order. Have a set prematch meal. Listen to the same music. Go to bed at the same time. Get a routine that is yours.

Coaches can assist athletes by:

A) Allowing the athletes to have input into some decisions. Including them in the plans.

B) Teaching them how to prepare mentally.

C) Encouraging them to take control of their preparation, and to have responsibility for being ready to wrestle.

How would you lose?

This might sound like a stupid question, but it's one that we need to ask ourselves. "When I lose a match, just how does it usually happen?" could be the smartest question you ever ask. One of the basic techniques for developing a winning program is to analyze what you need to do and then doing it. One of the ways we can do this is to investigate where you have been weak, or what you think might be an area of concern.

There is an interesting way of finding this information. It is called the "Where would you lose?" method. In this exercise, the athletes must decide where they are most likely to lose a match. From there, the athlete works to develop a remedy for whatever aspect of the match they have identified.

An example of this would be: a FS/GR athlete decides that he has been getting beaten because of fleeing the mat calls. He stays tough in the match, doesn't get turned, and doesn't get scored on, but always seems to get pushed out of the zone late in the match. The athlete should begin working on recognizing when he is in the zone. He builds a dialogue that initiates action when the athlete steps into the zone. "Zone! I need to drop my level, then drag or shuck back toward the center. Turn the corner. I control the zone!" He should actually practice a dialogue to help learn to respond in his matches.

A scholastic athlete seems to fall apart late in his match. He hangs tight until the last minute, and then gets scored on, or is scored on in overtime. "I give out." This athlete should look into his conditioning program, and then begin some fatigue control work. He might need to add an extra conditioning period to his practice, or learn a little pain/fatigue control. He could then make a dialogue that covers this aspect of his match.

By careful analysis of your match you can identify problem areas. By identifying these areas and then designing appropriate practices or methods to remedy these tendencies, you can remove many of them and make yourself more likely to make the match an honest battle.

So, how would you lose? Write a description that explains how you have lost any matches.

Are there any similarities between the ways you have lost these matches? If there are similarities, then how can you correct any problems that have appeared?

Perfect match ideas from the studs!

Let's look at some ideas from our World Class athletes to see what they think.

Kurt Angle-- *"I shake hands. High intensity right away. Hit a double leg and drive him out of bounds. 1 point and a caution. Par tarre-quick start to a gut wrench."* Later in the match--*"he needs to score, so I fake and move to create bad shots for him so I can score."* As Kurt closes his match-- *"Keep high tempo. Stay in the center. Strong defense, but stay aggressive. Shoot high crotch as he walks in unexpectedly."*

Matt tells us-- *"Good start. Get one hand in and get good lock. Right position for gut-wrench. Head in the middle and knees off the mat. Try to lock a hip and drive forward. Left side first then right. After gut, try lift or front head lock."*

Dennis Hall-- *"I used to prepare for competition without a consistent warm-up. My mind used to wander on me. During my old warm-up I used to think about what my opponent would be coming after me with. Now all I think about is doing my particular warm-up. When I step on the mat now, I am ready to go."*

Coach Doug Reese interviewed Hall and found that Dennis likes to wrestle a hard five minute match before he competes. Reese says, "In essence, Dennis finishes the equivalent of an entire wrestling match as part of his warm-up routine before he actually steps on the mat for a true competition."

"The reason I go hard before my first match is because--what match is usually your worst match? The first match! I have never seen anybody ever get a good first match. I feel much better getting the first match out of the way before a tournament even starts. I wrestle much better physically after a structured warm-up. Now I am ready to wrestle."

Solutions to problems

Now look at the different aspects of your total competitive experience, identify the problem areas, and then detail some solutions to the problems.

Week of the competition
What is the most pressing problem you see with your preparation? How do you plan to solve it?

Support group
What is the most pressing problem that could be helped by your support group? How do you plan to solve it?

How would you lose?
What is the most pressing problem you see occurring in your matches? How do you solve it?

What's the second most pressing concern in each of these areas?
Week of competition?
How would you solve it?

Support group?
How would you solve it?

How would you lose?
How would you solve it?

Good. Now, for a final thought: what would interfere with you completing your solutions to each of your concerns? If you can think of any, solve them! Once you learn to identify the problem, then quickly design a solution. You will see a change in the way you approach things. Nothing can scare you now, for you now know you can solve any problem!

Your perfect match finalized

It is time to pull all of your ideas together to form your perfect match. When you started, you probably didn't know there was so much information or ideas involved with the mental side of wrestling. That's okay. Now you do and you are ready to finalize your plan, learn it, make it become part of your automatic belief system, and then forget about it!

Just think. You are now many times better than you were before you started this work, and what is exciting is that you are now many times better than your opponents. You have been through several activities. You have learned some new ideas and brushed up on some things that you already knew. You have been introduced to psychological concepts and even have thought about some wrestling strategies. Now, get your ideas together, and let's plan your perfect match.

What do you want to think in each of these situations?
Week of your competition:

Morning of (as you get up):

At the gym:

Warming-up:

As you walk to the mat:

As you shake hands:

Your first contact:

Your first flurry:

Top:

Bottom:

Feet:

How will you overcome problems?

What are some of you plan B's?

Remember, a perfect match is one where you beat a top notch opponent by doing things right. Make your "perfect match" a tough, hard fought battle that is close, or goes into overtime. Include him scoring, so that you will develop a dialogue to battle that situation. (My elite guys usually end up writing three to four pages.)

Match tape and relaxation script

Many of my athletes train their perfect matches by using an audio tape. You can do the same. It just takes a little planning. Write your ideas and dialogue for each section just as you did in your perfect match. Have in mind some music and other thoughts that you want to hear. Then all you have to do is record your perfect match over your music. Dennis Hall listens as he drives his truck. Women's National Champ and 1996 Most Outstanding Women's Wrestler, Stephanie Murata listens as she warms up for her competition.

Include:
Perfect warm-up plan listing activities and dialogue.
List the things you want to think. Inspirational quotes.
Favorite actions or moves. Your prematch thoughts.
What is your prematch focus?
Pick your music. Each athlete has his own. Use music that will help you control your activation. If you want to "jack up", use fast, throbbing songs with a beat. If you want to calm down, then select classical pieces. Some of my athletes like rock, while others "Jock Rock", and some even like thunderstorms and rain. It is your choice.

Write and record it
Now write the script and then record it over your music. Listen to it whenever you want to get into your match! Repetition is the key to learning, so listen to it often. Dennis recommends five (yes five!) times a week.

Relaxation script
Sometimes experts make things seem more complicated than they really are. Relaxation is a state that we all know how to achieve. (We just didn't know what it was.) Think of a time when you decided to take a quick or short nap. You laid down and got comfortable, your body became heavy, you felt good, but you were not

exactly asleep. You still heard everything. You may have even been listening to your box, TV, or headphones. That is the state we are seeking. So you already know how to do it. I'll just give you a method to find that state of feeling any time you want it.

Kick back and relax

First, get comfortable. Find a quiet place to lie down, and then loosen your clothes. Take off your shoes. Undo your belt. Scan your body for tightness, and then scan it for relaxed areas. Focus on the relaxed areas. We want a feeling of calm, not really a "sleepy" feeling.

Next, anchor (mentally return) to a time when you were very tired. Capture that feeling of tiredness. Feel the ground or bed touching your body. Focus on that feeling and think about the physical sensation. Close your eyes. Think about that moment. Take a breath, deep and easy. Good. Now take another. As you blow it out, imagine a stream of tension leaving your body. Let your body go. It will settle into a nice, heavy, comfortable position.

Focus on you legs. Notice the sensation. Tell them to relax so much that they become heavy. Now, do the same with your hands. Your arms. Your neck.

Smile to yourself and think of a nice time in your life. Some of my athletes like to think of a air mattress floating on the Gulf. Others find a couch in front of a TV as the most relaxing. Think about a situation where you are totally comfortable and in control.

Focus on that feeling of calmness. Empty your mind of of thought words, and then replace them with feeling words. Relax, heavy, calm, light, relax, happy, calm, light. Focus on those feelings. Find the heaviest, most relaxed part of your body. Ask that feeling to spread across your body. Feel yourself getting heavier. Notice the floor, how it is beginning to lift you up. You can become so heavy that it feels as if the floor is lifting you. You should now be relaxed and calm. Enjoy it.

Focus on positive ideas, keep yourself in your zone and have a good time!

Simulation training
by Coach Doug Reese
USA Wrestling **Gold** Level Coach

Simulation training seeks to make your training environment as similar to the competition environment as possible. While mental skills training such as imagery relies on the use of imagination, simulation relies on the manipulation of the training environment by actually creating the stresses under which you will perform. Physical training develops the muscles and nerve pathways that are directly involved in the control or the muscles. Imagery is a very good way to continue to train and develop these nerve pathways in the brain.

Simulation, however, seeks to train all the parts of your brain and the body by helping you to physically perform the skills being trained under a physical environment that creates all the stresses and distractions of competition. This will help you to develop the mental skills that stop you from "choking under pressure." Simulation training will enable you to actually feel that you have been in this situation before.

Aspects of Simulation

You should try to introduce the following stresses into you own training session to make practice as realistic as possible.

1) Occasionally wrestle live matches in practice with a referee. Dress in your singlet. Go through your pre-match rituals. Check in, walk to the center, shake hands and wait for the whistle!

2) Every opportunity should be taken to train in the worst conditions possible for competition. Practice in a variety of conditions. Replicate every type of condition--from high heat and humidity with a lack of air conditioning to a cold gym with no heat.

3) Push yourself to perform effectively when fatigued so that you can learn how to concentrate on perfect technique and position when your physical reserves are low.

4) Train when you have just eaten. This helps you cope with the consequences of having to perform effectively if called to the mat unexpectedly.

5) Train just after cutting weight. You will often have to perform in this situation.

6) Get used to training in the morning. Most wrestling tournaments start at 9:00 to 10:00 a.m.. You must be able to get going, full out, at this time of day. Eat what you would normally eat prior to an actual competition that begins in the morning.

If you simulate conditions that are much worse than the real conditions under which you will perform, then you will have some very strong advantages. These advantages can include:
1) confidence that you can handle anything thrown at you.
2) well-practiced skills to handle the stresses and distractions of competition.
3) confidence in your stamina and the ability to keep technique at a high skill level even under less than ideal physical conditions such as fatigue, sickness, poor facilities, poor environmental conditions, etc.

You may not have all the resources at your disposal to use all the aspects of simulation in your own personal training sessions, but you should be able to incorporate some of these ideas effectively into your training routine to help you prepare to give a maximum performance under difficult physical and psychological conditions.

Post Test

Has it been a good trip through these pages? Take this post test to see how much you have learned. You can check your progress by comparing your pretest answers to what you know now.

1. What is *sport psychology*?
2. Name *two application methods* for sport psych work
3. What is the *arousal* theory (also called activation)?
4. What is *focus*?
5. What is *simulation*?
6. What is *stress*?
7. Explain *morphing*.
8. List the three types of *self-talk*.
9. List the *three major concerns that build stress*.
10. Name *two types of goals*.
11. Goals should be _____, _____, _____ and _____ if they are to be effective.
12. Explain the two ways *stress* can show itself.
13. What is *centering*?
14. What is *flow*?
15. What are *affirmations*?
16. What are *support groups* and how do they help?
17. What is the difference between *relaxation, visualization, imagery,* and *simulation*?
18. What is *insomnia*?
19. How does one handle *adverse conditions*?
20. How does a team hold a *mental skills practice*?
21. After the competition, what should a coach or athlete do?
22. What are the *strategies* for your style and weight?
23. Explain how you can use *audio tapes* to improve your performance.
24. How does the story "Goldilocks" fit into your planning?

Closing

You are the master of your future and you already possess the skills for success. Achieving this success will boil down to how well you put all of the parts of your training program together for your competitions. As a coach, all I can do is offer you help and suggestions. You must master the skills, and then perform.

If you have the discipline to follow through on this program, I wish you luck and hope you continue your successful ways. Drink from the fountain of knowledge. Take what you need. Balance the suggestions with what you already know. If the ideas make sense, then incorporate them into your belief system. If they don't, then strengthen your belief in what you already know. The keys to success are on your chain.

Coach Steve Fraser, our National Greco-Roman Head Coach says that we should: **Expect to win!** But to do that you must make sure you do the things it takes to be a winner. That makes it much easier to be confident in your expectations.

Sayings from the wise
Beazor the wise
1) Once the words have been spoken, the deeds must be done.
2) Success is a journey, not a destination.

Victory Secrets of Atilla the Hun, by Wess Roberts
1) Weak chieftains, when faced with confrontation, often do the easiest thing---nothing!
2) Because warriors accept competition as an inevitable part of life, they look for ways to excel at it.
3) When attacking, chieftains exploit the enemy's weaknesses first--unless, by intelligent maneuvering or brute force, they can neutralize the enemy's strengths.
4) Winning is as much a habit as an outcome.

Resources and credits

I have been doing this for so long that many of the ideas I use were learned years ago and I can't properly attribute them. For that I am sorry. But to my fellow writers and coaches who have contributed knowledge to this work--I offer you my thanks!

Foundations of Sport and Exercise Psychology. Weinberg and Gould. (1995) Human Kinetics. Champaign, IL.
Sport Psychology Interventions. Shane Murphy. (1995) Human Kinetics. Champaign, IL.
The Art of War, by Sun Tzu. Translated by Yuan Shibing. (1990). Sterling Publishing. New York, NY.
The Mental Athlete. Kay Porter and Judy Foster. (1986) Ballantine Books. New York, NY.
Thinking Body, Dancing Mind. Huang and Lynch. (1992) Bantam Books. New York, NY.
Victory Secrets of Attila the Hun. Wess Roberts. (1993) Doubleday. New York, NY.
Wrestle To Win! Beasey Hendrix. (1996) High Performance Athletics. Marietta, GA.

Special thanks to:
World Champion and Olympic Silver Medalist Dennis Hall who is an inspiration to many of our Greco wrestlers.
USAW Gold Level Coach Doug Reese for his and his athletes' help in learning how to apply this program to teams.
Olympic Greco-Roman Gold Medalist and National Greco Coach Steve Fraser for trusting in my program and inviting me to work with the National Program.
Olympic Gold Medalist and World Champion Kurt Angle.
Olympic Gold Medalist Kendall Cross.
Olympic Silver Medalist Matt Ghafarri.
Olympic Greco-Roman Head Coach Rob Hermann.
Greco-Roman World Team Coach Dan Chandler.
USAW National Coaches Education Director Brett Penager.
Coach Bill Martell.
Our National coaching staff.
USA Wrestling's national staff.
And to all of the athletes who listened to, answered and suffered through all of my questions, surveys, and handouts.

Coach Beasey Hendrix

Coach Hendrix has enjoyed success in several areas of the sport. A two-time Olympic Team Trials Finalist in freestyle, his clubs and school teams have produced over 20 Junior-aged All-Americans in scholastic, freestyle, and Greco-Roman wrestling.

In 1995, he became USA Wrestling's third "Gold Level Certified Coach". (The first under USA Wrestling's new coaches certification program.) A nationally known clinician, Hendrix has an Educational Specialist Degree, and a Masters in Psychology.

He has published over 2 dozen articles on mental skills for athletes and he is author of **Wrestle To Win!** a book on basic mental skills for wrestling.

You may see him working with national team members at the Olympic Training Center (where he has presented over a dozen seminars), in prematch preparation, or even in their corners during their matches. In 1996, he was selected as the "psychological skills coach" for the US Greco-Roman Olympic Team. He has consulted with athletes from around the World, including Scotland, Botswana, Germany, Canada, Nigeria, Quatar, Uganda, Puerto Rico, England, Iceland and Bulgaria.

Major accomplishments:

US Greco Olympic Team psychological skills coach. (1996).
Team Leader. US National Greco Tour to Sweden. (1997).
Two time US Olympic Team Trials Finalist.
Wrestling USA National Hall of Fame.
WUSA "National High School Assistant Coach of the Year".
USA Wrestling Gold Level Coaches Certification. (1995).
WUSA "Georgia Man of the Year".
Georgia Athletic Coaches Association "State Assistant Coach of the Year". (4X).
GACA "Area Coach of the Year" (Cross Country-6X).
Who's Who Among America's Teachers. (1990-94).
USA Wrestling Bronze Level Coaches Instructor.
USAW Silver Level Coaches College Instructor.
National H. S. Athletic Coaches Convention Speaker.

Consultant: USA Freestyle and Greco World Teams.
Consultant to numerous university teams.
Authored more than 25 articles for over a dozen magazines.
Mental skills consultant to Olympic athletes in several
    sports.
Named "Coach", "Man", or "Assistant Coach of the Year" over
    two dozen times by seven different organizations.

**1996 US Olympic Greco-Roman Wrestling Team
Coach Hendrix stands proudly among America's
best Greco-Roman wrestlers.**

Photo courtesy of USA Wrestling

 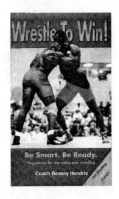

Order form for books

Please send me _____ copies of:

Wrestle Your Perfect Match!
A program for designing
your own perfect match.

I have enclosed $11.95 plus $3.00 shipping and handling (Georgia residents add 5% tax) to:

High Performance Athletics
P.O. Box 669364
Marietta, Georgia 30066
(Write for team discounts when purchasing 15 or more.)

Name_____

Address_____

City/State/Zip_____ _____ _____

Phone number:_____-_____-_____

Another book by Coach Hendrix:
Wrestle To Win!
Be smart. Be Ready.

Coach Hendrix goes into detail about mental skills preparation for athletes. Nearly 200 pages of suggestions and ideas will help you understand mental skills for wrestling. ($13.95 + $3 s&h)